P. R Hanrahan

Echoes of the Past

Odes on Ancient Ireland, national melodies, and other miscellaneous pieces

P. R Hanrahan

Echoes of the Past

Odes on Ancient Ireland, national melodies, and other miscellaneous pieces

ISBN/EAN: 9783337322663

Printed in Europe, USA, Canada, Australia, Japan

Cover: Foto ©ninafisch / pixelio.de

More available books at **www.hansebooks.com**

ECHOES OF THE PAST

Odes on Ancient Ireland, National Melodies,
and other Miscellaneous Pieces.

BY

P. R. HANRAHAN

AUTHOR OF "EVA," ETC.

DUBLIN
M. H. GILL AND SON
50 UPPER SACKVILLE STREET
1882

PREFACE.

MANY of the following songs and poems were composed in leisure moments, many years ago, at an early age, and others have been continued, at intervals, to the present time. I am fully sensible that the public taste for poetry has much declined since the days of Moore, Byron, and Scott; but I am also persuaded that a strong poetical taste always exists in the world, particularly for the young; for it is, or ought to be, the exponent of fine feelings, elevated ideas, and deep national sympathies, which no one will say exist only in the past; and I am disposed to believe that it only requires a hand to touch the chords with enthusiasm and devotion to produce a tone at once responsive and effective as those of a former day.

PREFACE.

The Author is painfully sensible of the temerity he incurs in entering a path lighted up by the brilliancy of Moore, the fire and energy of Byron, and the charming simplicity of Scott; but he feels his efforts will not be altogether useless if he succeed in evoking a love of country where that sentiment lies dormant, or in alleviating a single pang when pain and sorrow oppress the heart.

P. R. HANRAHAN.

Farnogue Cottage, Wexford.
    February, 1882.

CONTENTS.

SONGS OF NATURE.

	PAGE
Songs of Nature. No. 1	9
Songs of Nature. No. 2	13
Songs of Nature. No. 3	16
Songs of Nature. No. 4	20

SABBATH SONGS.

The First Sabbath. Scene.—The Garden of Eden	29
The Sabbath Morning. Scene.—Ireland	30
The Sabbath Day. Scene.—Rome	33
The Sabbath Evening	38
The Last Sabbath. Scene.—Heaven	40
To my Guardian Angel	44
The Angelus Bell	46
Old Times	48

LABOURERS' LAYS.

I've heard there's a Stranger	51
The *Times'* Commissioner	53
The Homes of Ireland	54
Is there a Heart in Erin's Isle?	56
Song of the People	57
The song of the Irish Artisan	58
Dear Land	60
A Ballad of 1847	62

NATIONAL MELODIES.

Men of Wexford	65
Bright, bright was the morn	67
Oh! blame not the men	69
By Slaney's Banks	71
Sing me that little song again	72
The Wish	73
Song	75
Can the Church of God be blighted?	76
The English Poor-House	77
Bring back, bring back	79
Oh! Erin of the Mountains	80
To a Mountain Fern	81
O Kathlin! sing that song again	83
Wake! Erin, wake!	84

CONTENTS.

	PAGE
The Summer is come back again	86
To Mary O'Donnell	88
The Irish Mother's Lament	90
The Emigrant's Farewell	91
Awake, ye Bards	94
The Old Churchyard	96
Sing on, sing on	99
The Fetch	99
Listen to the Fairies singing	101
The Banshee's Song	102
To Erin	103
Stanzas to Erin	108
Weep no More	110
Speak softly	111
The Invader	112
Song from the "Dead Man's Chair"	115
Come let us pledge	119
A Lament for not knowing the Irish Language	121
To S.	124
The Vision.—Part First	125
The Vision.—Part Second	127
I love the songs of Ireland	130

SENTIMENTAL SONGS.

I cannot sing of love to-night	132
O Kathleen! guard, oh! guard thy Heart	133
Oh! turn away those eyes of light	134
Child of clay	136
To Mary, after a long absence	137
My own dear girl	138
I saw thy kindling beauties shine	139
The days of youth	140
"Go not away"	141
Though feeling	143
Oh, would I were a child again	144
When the first smiling beams of day	145
Oh! wilt thou give me back my heart?	147
To Agnes	148
To M.	149
Stanzas	150
Stanzas to * * * *	152
Oh, think of me!	153
There's none like thee	154
I met thee in life's early prime	155
Come wander by the Valley's Well	156

CONTENTS.

	PAGE
Never! oh, never	157
Lines to * * * *	159
Sonnet to Mary	161
To * * * *	161
Farewell	164
May	166
Come, wend our way	168
The songs of childhood	169
To * * * *	171
To * * * *	172
Woman's Eye.—To Jane	173
Song.—One last look	175
Fitzstephen's song	176
When last I met thee	177
Stanzas	179
Lost Days	181
I had one friend	183
An Evening Thought	185
To Mirza, with a present of early Flowers	186
Maid of Erin	187
Lines on burning a package of letters	189
Additional Stanzas	191
The Sea-boy's Grave	193
How oft in the evening	195
An Acrostic	196
To Josephine	197
To Eliza	198
On presenting a Four-leafed Shamrock	200
Lines to * * * *	201
Oh! turn again	202
Lines to Mirza	203
An Acrostic	205
Lines to * * * *	205

OCCASIONAL PIECES.

Sunrise	207
Lines written by Moonlight	208
An Acrostic	210
Lines written in "Childe Harold"	210
Stanzas on the Very Rev. J. L. leaving Wexford	211
Lines on visiting Brown's Castle	212
Written by Moonlight in Ardcolm Churchyard	214
Written after visiting the Grave of "Rosaloo"	215
A Tribute to the Memory of "Donald of Shielmaliere"	217
Stanzas inscribed to "Glenalvon"	219

CONTENTS.

	PAGE
To a Friend, on his leaving the country	221
My old Companions	222
Lines on Temperance	226
Lines written after an evening's walk	227
To R. R., Waterford, on presenting him with a Copy of my Poems	230
To a young Oak	232
On the death of Mrs. C.	234
On the death of an interesting infant	235
To Lizzy in Heaven	236
The Poet's soul is always sad	238

MISCELLANEOUS PIECES.

The African Wilderness	239
To "Raymond of Forth"	241
To A. C.—An apology for not attending an Evening Party	246
On an old House	247
Additional lines, written twenty years after	250
To a Tear	251
A Prologue	252
The Idiot Boy to his Widowed Mother	253
The Wail of the Spirit of the Churches of Ireland	255
The Seraph's Song	257
The Depopulated Village	260

ODES OF ANCIENT IRELAND.

Ode I.—To hear the Minstrels once more play.—Introductory	267
Ode II.—A Prelude.—The Song of the Last Senachie	270
Ode III.—The Milesian Expedition to Ireland	272
Ode IV.—The Milesians' Morning Hymn	275
Ode V.—The Milesians sail for Ireland	276
Ode VI.—The Milesians' Evening Hymn	278
Ode VII.—The Storm	280
Ode VIII.—After the Storm.—The Landing	281
Ode IX.—The First Battle.—The March	283
Ode X.—The Engagement	284
Ode XI.—The Princess Scota's Burial	289
Ode XII.—The Dirge	291
Ode XIII.—The Enchanted Palace of the De Danaans	295
Ode XIV.—Tailton	299
Ode XV.—The Spell	302
Ode XVI.—The Last Battle	308
Ode XVII.—The Conclusion	320
Notes	325

Echoes of the Past.

ECHOES OF THE PAST.

Songs of Nature.

No 1.

"Every field is like an open book; every painted flower hath a lesson written on its leaves."

OH, glorious Nature! thou art sure to please
In every clime: thy hills, thy vales, thy seas
Are full of wonder, majesty, and Thee,
Divine Creator. Thus I bend the knee
To thy fair temples—Earth, Sky, Ocean, Air—
Go where we will Omnipotence is there !
The blazing lightning's fork'd and lurid flash,
The bursting thunder's deep-toned rattling crash;
The storms careering through the murky air,
Or golden sunshine calmly sleeping there;
The wild waves playing in their stormy mirth,
The "big rain" dancing to the thirsty earth;

The cataract rushing with tremendous force,
The bright rills creeping o'er their pebbly course :
The pearly dew-drops shining on bright flowers,
Thy spicy breezes and thy shady bowers;
Thy painted bow, deep in yon azure heaven,
Thy dewy twilight shed at parting even ;
Thy morning's glories, and thy mid-day beam,
The pale moon trembling o'er a silver stream;
And night hung round with planet-worlds on high,
Serenely gleaming through her ebon sky—
All these are lovely, and all Nature's these !
Then let us wander where the spicy breeze
Fans the bright bowers of the Cyclades ;
Thence to the Poles, and to the burning line—
Roam where we will the features are divine.
Like the wild bee, that hums about the bloom
Of every flower, and sips at its rich perfume,
So will we fly to every land and find
As sweet a banquet in the reasoning mind.
First, let's to China, where young morning sighs,
'Midst opening rosebuds, till he steals their dyes,[1]
And thus reflects them like a ruby kiss
On his bright brow, and smiles around in bliss.
To either Tartary, where people stray,
Where fancy pleases o'er the grassy lea ;
Now through the vale where crystal waters glide,
And now upon the mountain's thymy side,
They tend their flocks, and as they pass along,
Their journey's lightened by some tale or song—

Strangers alike to acts and politesse,
They lead a life of ignorance and bliss.
To Tibet, where the Himalayas rise,
Dark, shadowy, ethereal, to the skies—
So vast, so awful, profound, the soul
Imbibes emotions we cannot control ;
We feel our own contracted littleness,
A speck, an atom in the great abyss.
Now let us rove where Ceylon's beauteous isle
In orient beams of day is seen to smile,
Where Birds of Paradise, in glorious dyes,
Usher young morning through the Indian skies ;
To India, blushing in the blaze of day,
A diamond sparkling in a coral bay,
Where Delhi's gorgeous palace, peacock-throne,
And golden palm unrivalled stand alone;
Where the broad Ganges "flows direct from heaven,"
Whose votaries worship, drink, and are forgiven ;
To Persia's plains, whose dark-eyed daughters dream
Their lives away by some enchanted stream,
Or tend their altars in some magic grove;
Their souls all rapture, and their hearts all love.
To Mount Caucasus, where the Georgian maids
And fair Circassians wander o'er the glades—
Formed but to love, nor knowing aught of crime,
Till rudely torn from their natal clime,
To cheer a while some tyrant's leisure hours,
Then left to wither like to virgin flowers,

Plucked from the parent stem to deck a hall
For a grand feast or solemn festival!
To happy Araby, whose incense-trees
Sheds clouds of fragrance on the passing breeze;
Where Asia Minor traces on her breast
A thousand towns for ever sunk to rest.
All there is changed—save Nature—she's the same,
Altered in nothing, but, perhaps, the name.
Thus kingdoms fall, and nations pass away,
Like dewdrops drunk up on a summer's day.
Yet, still the same, unchanged her mountains stand,
Through whose rough vistas see the Holy Land![2]
No voice of Timbrel comes from olive bower,
But silence deep and desolation lower,
As if but now to Babel's streams were swept
The maids of Juda, on whose banks they wept!
O Nature! thou in every clime hast charms—
Here soft and soothing, there thy strength alarms;
Now calm and quiet as an infant's sleep,
Then hurled in thunders o'er a boiling deep.
If there be one who do not feel thy power,
Whose sordid soul hath never passed an hour
Alone with thee from tumult and from noise,
He never knew aught of earth's purest joys.
Oh, how I loved thee, worshipped since a child,
And wandered forth through many a woodland wild,
Or wrapped in storm, in darkness, and in night,
I entered into all thy fierce delight,
Until my unchained spirit wandered free,
And I became, as 'twere, a part of thee!

No. 2.

> "O Nature, how in every charm supreme!
> Whose votaries feast on raptures ever new!
> Oh, for the voice and fire of Seraphim,
> To sing thy glories with devotion due!"
>
> BEATTIE.

NATURE, let's view thee on the Afric strand
Where ancient rivers roll o'er golden sand
Where Egypt, parent of young science, first
From primal night in all her glory burst;
Where broken temples, palaces, and fanes,
Tell what she was—'tis all that now remains.
To fierce Nubia, where no cooling breeze
Comes whispering through the feathery cocoa-trees;
No voice of streamlet babbling through its vales,
But sultry summer round the year prevails,
And king and peasant listlessly and calm,
Pass life away beneath the desert's palm;
Far to the south, see Abyssinia rise,
A cloud of perfume to the tropic skies—
There the broad Nile, in all its pride and power,
Comes calmly on through many a citron bower,
And "happy valleys" gleam like fairy isles,
Through flowery glades and aromatic wilds.
O'er wide Sahara's parched and burning sands,
No tree or flower in beauty there expands;
No vocal songsters flit through groves of balm,
But here and there a solitary palm

Waves its dark boughs against the Afric sky—
'Tis all of life that ever meets the eye,
Unless, perhaps, the ostrich-bird that's found
The sole possessor of that desert ground.
Still it is sublime in its vastness; there
Is proved the truth that "God is everywhere!"
See fruitful Guinea, teeming with delight,
Most rich in all that's grateful to the sight,
There mellow fruits in tropic lustre shine,
The citron, olive, and the luscious pine.
But hark! the fetters clank on hordes of slaves,
Whose life-blood flows upon their brothers' graves;
Or torn all bleeding from that village home
Where all his lifetime he was wont to roam,
Free as the birds upon the wilding spray,
As free from care and innocent as they!
Pleasant Nigretia, let me wander free
Through thy deep shades of ease and luxury,
And hear delighted at the close of day
The deep-toned howlings of the beasts of prey:
The Lion thundering through a thicket-brake,
The Jackall prowling round some forest-lake,
The Tiger panting in the verdant shade,
The Boa basking in the sunny glade,
The Vulture wheeling through the sultry sky,
The fierce Hyena's solitary cry:
All there is savage, solitary, grand,
The wildest feature in that burning land.

Through soft green trees, with fabled fruits of gold
View that bright land, Hesperides of old ;[3]
There, Fancy first ascended her bright throne,
Stern Truth then fled, and all remained her own ;
There shrined in tints most exquisitely wrought[4]
The Poet wandered through the realms of thought,
Till he the heavenly inspiration caught ;
Then soar'd away to Helicon's pure fount,
Which purified him for the " sacred mount."[5]
Barbary States !—there smiling nature plays
In silver sunshine o'er thy thousand bays ;
Eden of Afric—ancient classic land,
How sunk, how fallen ! 'Twas thy own bloody hand
That lighted first destruction's burning brand.
Now desolation sweeps thy crimson waves—
Thy chiefs were pirates, and thy people slaves.
Bright Freedom shrieked and fled thy hated shore
When Carthage fell and Hannib'l lived no more !
I pity those who pass their lives away
'Midst cities' din, who never saw the day
Break fresh and glorious over dewy flowers,
Nor evening stealing through her saffron bowers,
Nor moonlight sleeping on the silent glen,
Far, far away from tumult, noise, and men,
Who only know them through the poet's page,
Or scenic paintings of a narrow stage.

No 3.

"Magna opera Domini: exquisitata in omnes voluntates ejus."—PSALM cx.

FAR o'er Atlantic's broad and deep blue wave,
Land of the stranger, of the free, the brave—
Land of the Exiles' of the Patriots' grave,
Who fled the country that they could not save—
What, though no classic lore to thee belong
No ancient bards have poured their souls in song,
No mad ambition driven his sanguined car
Through thy broad plains, and wak'd the voice of war;
Though no rude temples of the pagan time
Hath found a place in thy too modern clime;
No ancient cities of a former age
Which live but now in the historic page:
All these are grand—but grandeur in decay
Speaks of what *was*, but now has passed away,
The light and glory of another day!
Thou hast the present! and its likeness there
In vain we seek for in the world elsewhere!
Fair, free Columbia, young world of the west,
Where sublime Nature sets her beauteous crest,
Where evening sunshine softly steals away
In "farewell smiles" o'er many an ocean bay;
Where lofty mountain's ring eternal peals
Of solemn thunder through her misty veils;
Where dark, deep woods in solemn silence wave
Their verdant bough above some nameless grave,

And beauteous birds flit here and there along
Through flowery bow with varied tones of song.
There rapid torrents dash their boiling brine
Down rugged rocks tremendous and sublime,
And circling wreaths ascend of rainbow spray [8]
As if young Nature kept a "Holiday!"
Lov'd land of wonders, thou art vast, immense,
The throne and temple of Omnipotence—
There let the Atheist wander and adore
The living God from thence for evermore.
For as we bend to worship at thy shrine,
Earth is forgot, the soul is all divine;
Eternal objects ever after fling
Their dreamy shapes o'er our imagining!
O'er the pale regions of the artic pole,
Where desolation waves her sable stole,
Where ocean monsters toss in foam the waves
And savage beasts prowl round thy sea-beat caves
And tempests chant the solemn funeral dirge
Of prostrate nature to the lonely surge,
Yet only there bright shapes of billowy light
Comes trembling through the inky dome of
    night, [9]
'Tis only there heaven's starry banner breaks
Through misty clouds o'er all thy icy peaks;
The land of lakes, half shining through her tears, [10]
Like some spoiled child of beauty, next appears:
There forest bloom primeval where the stroke;
Of woodsman's axe their silence never broke,

Nor human footsteps ever yet profaned
Thy blooming vales where only nature reigned,
Hail ye fair States ! where Plenty strews her horn,
Both Art and Nature thy broad plains adorn,
Here sparkling cascades, there the cedar-tree,'
Yonder vast vales of wealth and luxury,
And o'er thy pearl-waves Commerce with a smile
Invites each sail from every distant isle,
Where azure clouds hang o'er the glassy bay,
And every year is one long summer day,
There lies New Spain, adorned with every tree—
The sandal, rosewood, and mahogany.
Rich Quito sparkles with her silver caves,
Her golden mines and scarce less golden waves,
Eternal spring once bloomed among thy hills
From whose rough sides leaped many lovely rills,
Till earthquakes woke, and with despoiler's hand
Thick strewed destruction o'er the pleasant land. "
Peru and Chili next uprear their forms
Huge, vast, immense above the thunder storms,
And from their bright and dazzling domes of snow
Look down on warring elements below;
Mock suns ascend, and halos float in air,
As if the mountain spirit was at prayer !
The lava streams ! huge Cotopaxi sounds
Volcanic thunders through the vast profounds.
Buenos Ayres, where the Candar soars,[12]
In pride and beauty, o'er thy rocky shores,

And bright Potosi, with its thousand mines
Of gold and silver through bright foliage shines
Brazilian states, like some enchanted land
Of eastern tales, their sparkling gems expand ;
And De La Plata ripples over caves
Of spray crystal ere it meets the waves ;
Next Amazonia, far as eye can see,
Extends one lone, immense eternity,
So silent, shadowy, and still, 'twould seem [13]
As if creation lived but in a dream.
Bleak Patagonia's sterile rugged rocks
Are full of grandeur, through no brilliant flocks
From flowery vales pour forth the choral song
From morning's dawn throughout the whole day long.
Though spring scarce smiles upon that lonely clime,
Yet thy dark mountains rise bleak, wild, sublime,
Whose stormy caverns peal the thunder's chime,
And giant savages stalk o'er the land,
Like the creations of a wizard's wand, [14]
The broad Pacific, lit with many an isle,
Where " summer years and summer women " smile,
And dance beneath the Palm-grove's sacred shade
Young warrior chiefs, each with his favourite maid.
See western Indies fling their fragrant breeze [15]
Far o'er the coral groves of Carribees,
And moonlight's magic melt along the strand
Like paths of bliss that lead to fairy-land !
These are thy works, O Nature ! Let me be
Shrined in thy tints of light and harmony,
Till my wrapped soul forget mortality !

Oh, since such beauty, with unsparing hand,
Has been profusely scattered o'er the land,
Which is our home, at most, but a few years.
When it and all its grandeur disappears,
How glorious then must be that dwelling-place
Prepared for us above the realms of space
Upon which mortal eye could never gaze,
So purely bright is the ethereal blaze,
Which every moment flings fresh bliss around
The blooming vales of all that mystic ground—
A home to last forever—an abode
That satisfies the boundless mind of God.
Oh, where is the heart so cold, so hardened in
The ways of infidelity and sin,
As to ascribe to CHANCE these works that shine
Fresh from the GODHEAD's hand, eternal and divine!

No. 4.

"To me be Nature's volume broad displayed;
And to pursue its all-instructing page,
Or haply catching inspiration thence,
Some easy passage raptured to translate
My sole delight."—THOMSON.

NATURE, great parent of the Universe!
Thy flight's too daring for this humble verse—
Yet who can view thy kindling beauties melt
Without a tribute of what he had felt?

Though cold the language, unadorned the style,
Ah ! who could see Creation's glorious smile,
Her magic touches mirrored in the wave
That, trembling, back reflects the tints she gave;
Her circling seasons' ever-changing hue
For ever present, yet for ever new;
So slow, so gradual, her shadows blend,
'Twould seem without beginning, without end.
Thus solemn Winter, and young smiling Spring,
Rich roseate Summer, Autumn's golden wing,
All blend, and part, unite, and form a whole—
A choir of music bursting on the soul !
Who can see these all glorious, all divine,
Without the tribute of an humble line ?
At least I could not, cannot, though confess
These burning feelings I can ill express.
Greece ! glorious Greece, thy tuneful song is o'er,
And noiseless creep the waves upon the shore,
Thy patriot-chiefs in battles' bright array—
Thy feasts, thy shrines, thy temples—where are they ?
Thy feasts are gone, though still the sun doth kiss
His own lov'd temple, the Acropolis.[16]
The only worshipper that lingers there,
Of all her thousands who had knelt in prayer !
The rude barbarian with a merciless hand,
Flung desolation o'er that lovely land ;
The high-wrought column and the "breathing bust"
Are sadly shattered—trampled in the dust.

Thy sons were long in fetters, but the chain
Is broken now, and freedom wakes again.
While all thy former splendour's faded gone,
The glorious sunshine brightly glows still on
The same as when the Spartan heroes stood,
Who died Thermopylæ in patriot blood.
The clustering isles light up the amber waves
Like ocean stars, and through their dipping caves
Phosphor and purple shine, a flashing spray,[17]
Or calmly glide into some orange bay.
Turkey, thou'rt splendid even in decay!
What though thy glories faded, passed away,
Bright recollection, like a sunbeam's smile,
That fondly lingers o'er some ruined pile,
Still throws its glories round each hallow'd spot
That cannot, could not, ne'er shall be forgot.
Where Adrian waves sleep in the moonlight ray
A fairy city rises o'er the sea;
So silent, shadowy, and still it seems
Like a bright vision in the land of dreams!
Region of romance where young hearts do feel
The power of love, and care not to conceal
One burning thought, nor make one smile the less,
But raptured cling to love and loveliness.
The song, the gondola, and sparkling oar,
That swiftly glide along the winding shore;
The moonlight mask, the lute's soft breathing tone,
The still, sweet hour, when lovers meet alone,

Above them heaven, below the Lido's wave,
Nought else to see the secret pledge that gave
Hope to the timid, rapture to despair,
Bliss to the heart that finds its mistress there ;
Yes, Venice, romance, love, and song are thine,
Of which thou art the city and the shrine.
Fair Italy, steeped in rich mellow dyes,
With flowery landscapes, and with glowing skies,
The might and magic of thy former days
Are mingled with religion's purer blaze.
Rome, the Eternal, o'er thy shrine we trace
Jehovah's temple, throne, and dwelling-place ;
Here the dark Apennines their pine-trees wave
Above some lovely and neglected grave.
Yonder rude cross marks where some victim fell,
Above those chestnuts see the convent bell,
This mountain pass where the wild chamois bounds,
The hunter's hut that craggy summit crowns—
Vesuvius there wrapped in a flood of flame,
Like Sinai's top when spoke the Eternal's name.
O Italy ! where'er thy pilgrim strays
Remembrance throws her rich and mellow rays
Over each scene, like thy own evening skies,
Or childhood's half-remembered melodies !
Sublime, romantic, free-born Switzerland
Whate'er is bright, or beautiful, or grand
Is thine by Nature bounteously given.
The rugged rocks with thunders scathed, riven,

The gurgling cascade flashing in the gleam—
The deep, dark glen, the winding mountain's stream,
The calm lake sleeping in the evening beam,
The valley shining like a paradise,
Mont Blanc's high summit crowned with fields of ice,
Where thundering avalanches burst and break
And glaciers gleam on Rosa's topmast peak.
Germanic States, in your broad blooming land,
A rich variety of scenes expand;
Here Nature smiles with an enchanting grace,
And there a tear bedews her frozen,
Now dark, deep woodlands, now the purple vine
Luxuriant deck the lovely banks of Rhine.
Prussia, amid thy forest bleak and bare,
Though wintry wildness mostly lingers there
There is a grandeur, sublimity,
A solemn, savage, wild immensity!
Ah, Poland! thou the noblest, bravest, best,
Destruction trampled on thy bleeding breast;
Dismembered, torn in fetters, bleeding bound,
Let Pity's self draw Death's dark drapery round.
Behold bleak Russia, sterile, wild, and bare,
Where scarce one flower scents the chilly air,
Wild moss lies scattered o'er thy barren moor,
Huge rocks of ice gleam on thy frozen shore,
The stunted birch, the tall and tapering pine,
The mountain ash round which the lichens twine;

The reindeer sledge that skims the frozen lake,
Or lightly glides along the snowy flake;
And now is heard the thundering crash and roar
Of icebergs breaking on the Lapland shore.
Industrious Holland, where the waves have been
Now hamlets peep through bowers of brightest green,
And flowery arbours from deep fragrant shades
Where careless stray thy large and dark-eyed maids.
See, level Denmark, through refracted light,
Comes soft and scintillating to the sight,
Like moonlight lands appearing far away,
When viewed beneath her fading crescent ray.
Land of wild legends, where the Norsemen bold
Spread war and terror o'er each State of old;
Land where the "Sea Kings" long had ruled the deep,
And held dark council in their rocky keep;
Where from the mountain's craggy, wild recess
The red flame flashes of the Pythoness;
With magic drum the mystic spell is cast,
And demons dance around the whirlwind blast.
In that lone isle, far in the northern world,
Where Geyser boils, and where Mount Heckla burned,[18]
There nature partly draws aside the veil,
As if in pity she would half reveal
Her sublime secrets to admiring eyes,
Which vainly strive to read her mysteries.

Gay, glittering France, in thy soft, glowing clime
Bright summer tints play round thee; there the vine,
With clustering branches, twine around each bower,
Where dance her maidens in the twilight hour:
Sylph-like and silent they glide to-and-fro
Beneath the blossoms, as a fairy show.
Proud Spain, thy days of chivalry are gone,
And romance lights no more thy knight-errant on;
The tilt, the tournament, the long array
Of mail-clad warriors, glistening in the ray,
No more are seen—they all have passed away.
But still the dark-eyed, dark-haired Spanish girl,
With lips of rosebuds and with teeth of pearl,
Wakes her guitar from some sequestered bower,
And dreams of love in that enchanting hour,
When its own planet rises clear and bright
Upon the calm and cloudless summer's night.
Home of the Highlands, and of verdant hills,
Of deep, dark valleys, and of mountain rills,
Of woodland wilds, and lovely elfin sports,
Of foaming waterfalls, and lovely grots,
Where the aged Seer, through clouds of mist and spray,
Views the dim records of a future day;
How of thy chieftains and thy clansmen saw
The "fiery cross" blaze over copse and shaw? [19]
How oft thy hill-tops shone with beacon light,
That summoned all to meet for freedom's fight;

And all obeyed;—they lived but to be free,
Nor paused one soul 'twixt death and victory!
But now the spirit of that glorious day
Is, like thy heroes, long since passed away:
No Bruce nor Wallace may again return
To lead to victory and Bannockburn.
Imperious England, " mistress of the seas,"
From Cape Lopatka to the Carribees,
All own thy power where'er thy banner flies,
Be it in eastern or in western skies;
But she who nobly sets the captive free
Is still the foe to heaven-born liberty!
Although the slaves are free who touch thy strand
Freemen are chained where'er the Britons land!
Yes; burning homesteads, altars overturned,
Have marked their conquest over all the world. [20]
Oh, England, England, there is scarce a crime
Thou wert not guilty of in every clime:
Bear witness every land from Erin's isle
To Afghan's cities left a blazing pile.
Thy sons are brave, adorned with every art,
But these have steeled, not purified the heart;
Thy daughters fair but faithless, and thy wealth
The only shrine at which thy millions knelt.
My own lov'd Erin, " thy enchantments still
Are with me, round me, wander where I will."
Thou wert the Eden of the western wave,
A land of loveliness that freely gave

Its light and lustre to far distant lands,
Instead of warfare and of hostile bands.
Thou wert once sacred—oh, yes! still thou art,
And ever shall be to the Irish heart!
Though Slavery's footprints still are on thy brow,
Oh! never wert thou lov'd so much as now;
And voices rise above the tempest's roar,
On hill and valley, mountain-top, and shore.
Sublime thy matin thunders out before
Both men and angels : " We'll be slaves no more!"
And slaves no more is echoed far and wide
By peaceful millions far across the tide,
'Till distant nations catch the joyous sound,
And "Slaves no more!" through every clime resound!

Sabbath Songs.

No. 1.

THE FIRST SABBATH.

(*Scene.—The Garden of Eden.*)

The fair new world, all blooming like a bride,
Joy in her smile, and heaven by her side,
Without a stain to dim her radiant face,
Or check the flow of God's celestial grace,
Ere sin had come to quench the living light,
Before whose glory sunshine now seems night,
Rose fresh and sparkling from her native spars,
Like the young planet 'mid her sister stars.
And as the Sabbath threw its orient beams
O'er Eden's hills and consecrated streams,
Soft music woke a thousand echoes there,
As Adam first adored his God in prayer;
And while he knelt, sweet exhalations sent
Their wreath of fragrance to the firmament;
The solo ceased, and then there came a strain,
Such as on earth can never come again;
Sweet hallelujah's burst from flower and tree,
And boughs and branches waved in ecstasy!

The sunbeam first his pearly offering made,
As o'er the rose he counts his dewy bead;
Next sportive zephyrs glide through groves and bowers,
Loaded with offerings from immortal flowers,
Whose freshness fades not, for each night renews
Their bloom and beauty with celestial dews;
Old ocean, smiling, throws about his spray,
Like burning incense on a holiday!
Strange birds of every dye, a beauteous throng,
Pour forth their souls in one melodious song!
Beasts warr'd not with their kind, for then one soul,
One universal love, controll'd the whole.
And as all Nature poured her soul in praise
There shone a bright and clear seraphic blaze
From gems and gold, which then neglected lay
Like shells and corals in an eastern bay,—
And thus was kept the world's first Sabbath-day!

No. 2.

THE SABBATH MORNING.

(Scene.—Ireland.)

Who has not rejoiced when, the Sabbath appearing,
   Full of lustre and light, through the clouds of the east,
Like the Spirit of God when o'er chaos careering,
   He made thee, my own dearest Erin, the best,

The fairest, the happiest isle of the ocean,
   And gave to thy sons hearts as warm as brave,
Till the demon of discord reviled their devotion,
   And forced them to fly to the mountain and cave!
   Though plundered and torn, abandoned, neglected,
They clung to those shrines which their forefathers knew,
   And scarce had the Sabbath her glories reflected
On that hallow'd shrine ere they worshipped there too!

   Though Slavery's fetters were fastened around them,
They suffered in silence and did not rebel,
For tyranny tightened the trammels that bound them.
   If a poet or patriot dared but to tell
Of the days when her warriors, princes, and sages,
   Their banner of victory gaily unfurled;
When chivalry shone on their arms for ages,
   And Erin shed liberty over the world.[21]
And if in its anguish the spirit, half-broken,
   Would sigh o'er the wrongs of her overcharged breast,
'Twas the turbulent passions of rebels had spoken,
   And nought but the slave lash could lull them to rest!

Though the tempest for ages was gathering o'er them,
    One beacon still blazed through the long night of gloom,
Like the path of an angel it opened before them
    A vista of glory from heaven to the tomb!
Oh, yes; hallow'd land of my earliest affection,
    They tore from thee all the bright gems of the past,
But e'en in thy moments of deepest dejection
    Thy children clung to thy creed to the last.
In vain were the torches of fanatics lighted,
    In vain did they offer them freedom and gold;
Thy clergy and people were ever united,[22]
    Nor slavery nor torture could sever the fold!

But Liberty once more in smiles is returning
    To light up those shrines, hallowed even by time,
The Sabbath-bell peals, the sweet incense is burning,
    And the cross once more triumphs o'er all most sublime.
The young village girls in purity's dresses,
    With hearts full of love, on each festival day
Sing hymns to the "Boy-God" of Bethlehem to bless us,
    And all that is dear to us, dead or away.[23]
Oh, how lovely this scene after ages of anguish!
    United we triumphed o'er fanatic zeal;
O Erin, be firm once more, do not anguish,
    And thou'lt triumph o'er all that would dare to assail!

SABBATH SONGS.

No. 3.
THE SABBATH DAY.
(Scene.—Rome.)

I.

O MIGHTY Rome! thou who wert once the queen
    Of empires; thou whose eaglet-banners spread
Their gorgeous folds in triumph o'er the green
    Hill-tops of every land; thou who hast led
Thy conquering cohorts, whose majestic mien
    Caused terror to the bravest hearts that bled
For their lost country's freedom; thou art now
More potent than when empire crowned thy brow.

II.

What though the wide world's diadem is rent,
    And thy imperial sceptre passed away,
Though tower, palace, and proud battlement
    Have felt the influence of chill decay;
Oh! still there is a light from heaven sent
    More sublime far than all the bright array
That ever graced thy rich triumphal car,
Glittering with spoils from some inglorious war.[24]

III.

'Tis true the burning eloquence that rung
    In peals of thunder through the Senate's dome,
The poets' tongues that oft sublimely sung
    Of foreign war, or lashed some vice at home;

The classic feast, the mystic game which flung
   Their influence over philosophic Rome—
All these are gone, but in their place we see
Religion, pure, unsullied, holy, free!

IV.

No more the Priests' vestal lamp doth shine
   From marble halls around some idol-stone,
No more the blasphemies of rites divine
   Are paid to mortal on a dazzling throne, 25
Surrounded with his ministers of crime;
   No more the Gladiator's dying groan
Comes from the bloody circus where the gay
And princely meet to make a "Holy Day!"

V.

O God! where was thy forkèd lightning's flame?
   Why slept thy thunders in their murky shroud?
Where was the earthquake's devastating stream
   That hurled not vengeance on that haughty, proud,
And guilty city? No; one heavenly beam.
   Hath power over all that faithless crowd,
To turn their hearts from cruelty and vice,
And gently lead them on to Paradise!

VI.

A simple fisherman from Galilee,
   Whose little bark was all his earthly store,
And what he brought from that lone island sea;
   And often when the tempest lashed the shore,

The midnight moon would find him full of glee
   Returning home. Oh! it was *he* that bore
The light of life triumphant and unfurled,
The symbol of " Redemption to the world!"

VII.

As fades the night before the blaze of day,
   As melts the snow before the breath of spring,
So passed the pagan mummeries away
   Before the words of life. In vain they cling
To thrones and dynasties—these two give way,
   Until with loud hosanna's earth doth ring,
And kings and princes bend the suppliant knee,
And give their hearts, O GOD! alone to Thee.

VIII.

In vain old Tyranny stalks o'er the land
   In blood and carnage for three hundred years,[26]
In vain did Cæsars threaten and command,—
   Religion triumphed o'er all bonds and fears
From earth. Against them all she took her stand,
   And blazed the brighter 'mid her chains and tears,
Till pitying Heaven took her exiled child,
Wiped off her tears, and sweetly on her smiled.

IX.

And then she came out from the mountain-side,
   From the deep dungeon, and the wild recess,
More beautiful than an imperial bride,
   Though weeds and briers were her only dress;

Yet, as men gazed on her, the warm tide
  Of soft emotion—love and tenderness—
Flowed in upon the heart, till the wrapped soul
Bounded with joy and owned the soft control.

X.

And then men wondered how they could so hate
  And persecute this heavenly visitant;
And they resolved, before it was too late,
  To make amends for all their former want
Of love and duty. Then a throne of state
  They place her on, and on her brows they plant
The triple diadem, whose dazzling rays
Eclipse the splendour of Rome's brightest days.

XI.

As the rich rainbow, beautiful and bright,
  Extends an arch of peace through ambient air,
So does the prince and priest of God unite
  The earth with heaven, and all that's glorious there:
He, the connecting-chain, sparkling with light,
  As o'er it runs the electric flame of prayer;—
He, the one Supreme Head, to whom is given
The faith that fails not, but conducts to heaven!

XII.

There, changeless as the "everlasting hills,"
  She shines a beacon-light to every clime;
No tempests terrify, no storm fills
  Her with alarm. It is only crime

That throws a sadness o'er her, and distils
   The tender tear of pity many a time,
Scarcely less pure than that which angels shed
Above the dying Christian's guilty head.

XIII.

But, hark! what thunders shake Angelo's tower?
   What means that peal along the Tiber's side?
Why sounds the clarion as if hostile power
   Again appear'd in all their martial pride?
Why is each pathway strewed with branch and flower?
   Why is Saint Peter's portals opened wide?[27]
And why this grand and glittering array?
'Tis all to grace Rome's Christian Sabbath-day![28]

XIV.

And now, the assembled thousands are at prayer!
   Men from all climes and kingdoms:—here the Pole
Beside the Swiss, free as his mountain air;
   The dusky African pours out his soul
Next to the wild Circassian, white and fair;
   The faithful Irishman can scarce control
His feelings when, 'mid all that's great and grand,
He seems once more in his own lovely land.[29]

No. 4.

THE SABBATH EVENING.

Bright eve of beauty! oh, how sweet,
When earth and heaven seem to meet
And blend the loveliness that's here
With glory from the upper sphere,
Like smiles of tenderness that break
In sunshine o'er Devotion's cheek:
Yes; then 'tis sweet to watch the ray
Of the departing Sabbath-day;
To feel the spirit bounding high
In rapture to yon glowing sky;
To find the humble suppliant's prayer
Like exhaled perfume wafted there!
Who has not felt that soothing power
Of the soft tranquil evening hour?—
But language never can express
The magic of its loveliness!

The sunbeams sleep upon the hill,
The very winds and waves are still,
Where'er we turn, east or west,
It is a holy eve of rest;[30]
Above, beneath, on land and sea,
There shines a bright tranquillity.
The hymn of praise, the song of love,
From vale and bower rise above;

From lonely glens, from cities' throng,
There breathes the holy vesper song.
Here incense breathes and altar's shine,
And music too, rich, deep, divine,
Steals through the fretted aisles of light,
Like some celestial guardian sprite
That wanders in that holy hour
From his own amaranthine bower,
Whose presence, though unseen, doth throw
Around the heart a burning glow,
An ecstasy so fervent, deep,
And exquisite, that then to weep [31]
Is sweeter far, and holier, too,
Than all we ever felt or knew
Of earth-born pleasures, that will pass,
Like forms before a wizard's glass,
Leaving no trace or track behind,
Save in the troubled heart and mind :
A pang sometimes may settle there
Which leaves a wrinkled brow of care.
Now from each valley's wild recess
The accents of devotion bless ;
From lonely cottages doth rise
The hearts' sweet incense to the skies,
And hill and hamlet catch the strain,
And waft it back to heaven again ;
As when departing day-beams rest
In smiles upon the mountain's crest,

Like angels' footsteps, which imprint
Where'er they glide a glowing tint,
Reflecting back the light from heaven
Weaker, yet pure as when first given :
So from a world, e'en dark as this,
Ascend to the bright gates of bliss
Those prayer-notes far beyond the sky,
In one sweet heavenly melody !

No. 5.
THE LAST SABBATH.

(Scene.—Heaven.)

" And I saw a new heaven and new earth : for the first heaven and the first earth were passed away; and there was no more sea.

" And I saw the new Jerusalem coming down from God out of heaven prepared as a bride adorned for her husband.

" And I heard a great voice out of heaven saying, Behold the tabernacle of God with men, and He will dwell with them . . . And God shall wipe away all tears from their eyes ; and there shall be no more death, neither sorrow, nor crying; neither shall there be any more pain : for the former things are passed away " (Apoc. xxi. 1-4).

'Tis done !—and Earth, with all its hopes and fears,
Its joys and sorrows, all it holds most dear
And precious, all its pomps and pageantries
Have passed away like threads of gossamer.

All human passions, such as we feel them now,
Are dead :—ambition, wealth, and earthly love,
Which filled the world with tumult, is no more,
Save in remembrance, which, like a dream
Of long-forgotten things, scarce leaves a trace
On Memory's purified and polished shield.
And if at intervals a glance is cast
Across the yawning gulf which separates
Past from Present, Time from Eternity,
We then, sublimated and spiritualised,
With all our faculties transfused with light,
Shall view the pursuits of the present time
As we do now the playthings of childhood,
Which once absorbed our feelings and our thoughts,
Our very being, just the same as those
We deem of so much consequence at present.
The whole wide earth shall then God's temple be,
One vast expanse of many-coloured gems
Shining in rich, transparent brilliancy :
The jasper, sapphire, and the emerald,
The chrysolite, beril, and topaz blaze
With light, and melt and mingle all their hues
In ever-varying beauty. There no cloud
Nor vapour e'er shall float between our gaze
And heaven, whose bright and blissful regions
Shall then be filled with countless multitudes
Of glorious spirits, rising tier on tier,
And rank o'er rank in shining circles,
Up to the throne of the Omnipotent.

And first the Angels in celestial robes,
The least of whom is greater, more perfect,
And powerful than all the sons of men,
From Adam to the last of all his race.
The next above them the Archangels stand,
With glorious Michael shining at their head,
And Gabriel, like a cluster of bright stars,
Supports the other. Then the gorgeous Thrones,
The Dominations, and the mighty Powers ;
Through whom God's high omnipotence is felt
By all created things, fill the mid heavens.
Next, and higher still, the Principalities,
Who rule and govern in the courts above,
Extend through deep and long arcades of light
To blissful regions of immensity.
Above these shining hosts the Virtues next,
And nearer to God's high eternal throne
Are marshalled. There, in seven-fold rainbow tints,
They gush forth, like the fragrance of the rose,
The seven glorious gifts of the Most High
On all his creatures: Wisdom, Understanding,
Counsel, Fortitude, Knowledge, Piety,
And, greatest of them all, the Fear of God !
Then, through sweet regions of those alpine heights
Of glory the lov'd Cherubim, in troops
Of countless legions tune their golden harps
To perfumed notes of love through all eternity ;
While over all the blazing Seraphim,
Who know the most of all the sons of light,

Fill the empyrean courts around the throne;
But purest, greatest, highest of them all
The Queen of heaven sits enthroned in light,
Whose subtle beams extend through farthest space
Of those celestial mansions, and transfuse
Themselves in torrents of ecstatic bliss
O'er all creation and created things.
And then, along those endless, blooming vales,
And bowers of bliss a grand procession moves
Of countless multitudes in long array—
The sons of earth, the lov'd ones, the elect—
Chanting forth sweet hosannas, peal on peal,
In concert with the whole full choir of heaven,
Each moment adding torrents of delight
And new ecstatic raptures, till the soul
Can bear no more, no further weight of glory!
Then our more subtle senses, sight, and smell,
And hearing, pure, enlarged, intensified,
And in their light taking the other two
More carnal ones, are ever enlarging
Their capacity for increased delight!—
The eye is feasted with that glory
Which mortal vision ne'er could look upon
And live, nor " could the heart of man conceive;"
The ear is ever drinking in sweet notes
Of heavenly harmony, which flood the soul
With rapture; and, the sense of smell, so pure
And exquisite on earth, is here regaled
From flowers immortal in the blooming vales

Of paradise, which sigh their souls away
In adoration to the throne of light!
Thus all the senses, every faculty,
Such as we can conceive and feel them now
In all their strength as giving most delight,
Are ever filled with rapture, joy, and bliss,
Which never cloys, nor will admit of more
Enjoyment.   And thus, in heaven is kept,
Through endless ages, the last great *Sabbath-Day!*

No. 6.

TO MY GUARDIAN ANGEL.

OH, come, my angel-guard!—too long
   I've wandered far from God and thee;
And, guarded by the thoughtless throng,
The smile, the music, and the song,
I strayed, nor cared not right nor wrong—
   Alas! 'twas all alike to me!

When first young love in radiance came,
   He was so very well like thee,
I could not believe but 'twas the same
Bright form that hovered in a dream,
With smiles of bliss and soul of flame
   That dazzled and delighted me.

But soon the heart's gay trance was o'er
   And love no longer look'd like thee;
A nameless dread, ne'er felt before,
A sorrow festering at the core,
Too plainly told that heaven no more
   Looked with approving smiles on me.

I sighed, and called, and looked in vain,
   No glimpse of glory or of thee
Did ever bless my sight again!
But, oh! a deep and burning pain,
A ceaseless pang like guilt's own stain
   Fell like a withering blight on me.

I've often sought, in halls of light,
   To find a substitute for thee,
Where gems and flowers and eyes were bright,
And love, with all its magic might,
And wine cups shone before my sight,
   But nought could bring content to me.

Alas! for the poor giddy heart
   That sought contentment without thee!
Without a light, or guide, or chart,
How could it safely take a part
Where gaudly tinsel, glare, and art
   Too often cast there spells on me?

Then come, my angel-guard, too long
I've wandered far from God and thee!
Come! and no more the thoughtless throng,
The smile, the music, nor the song,
Shall ever warp this heart to wrong—
My angel-guard, thou'lt be with me!

No. 7.

THE ANGELUS BELL.

"There is always something pleasingly solemn in the custom, by which, at a melodious signal, every human being throughout the land unites at the same moment in a tribute of thanks to God for the mercies of the day."—WASHINGTON IRVING.

I.

Ave Maria! the Angelus bell
Sweetly floats on the morning air;
Ave Maria! what mystic spell
Has drawn the aged and young to prayer,—
A spirit there is in the sounds as they start,
For they send a thrill of joy to the lonely heart.

II.

Ave Maria! it passes along—
All hearts are uplifted in prayer:—
The old, the lovely, the weak and strong,
The guilty and guiltless are there;
The innocent child and the man of crime
All heard and felt the sweet Angelus chime.

III.

Ave Maria! the signal again
   At mid-day comes in sunny pride,
In the crowded city and lonely glen
   All earth-born thoughts are set aside,
And the weary workman pauses to pray,
And the tired traveller stops on his way.

IV.

Ave Maria! dark ages have passed
   Since the echoes of Erin gave
A response to the Angelus bell on the blast;—
   For then 'twas treason for the slave
To worship at the old national shrine
That his fathers taught him to believe divine.

V.

Ave Maria! the daylight departs,
   And once more the Angelus chime
Like a voice from heaven draws all hearts
   To prayer as in the olden time,
When rock and valley repeated the knell
As it rung out the parting day's farewell.

No. 8.

OLD TIMES.

"The moment the Christian expired the bell was tolled. Its solemn voice announced to the neighbourhood that a Christian soul had departed, and called on those who heard it to recommend his soul to the mercy of his Creator. All were expected to join, privately at least, in this charitable office, and in monasteries, even if it were the dead of night, the inmates hastened from their beds to the church, and sung a solemn dirge."—Dr. LINGARD: *The Anglo-Saxon Church.*

I.

OH! for the times, the good old times,
   When deep from the wooded dell,
At midnight, came the solemn chimes
   Of the old monastic bell,
Which summoned monk and anchorite
   Before the thrice holy shrine
There, with the worldling to unite
   In prayer to the throne divine :
For a soul hath passed through the realms of air ;—
Come, brothers, all join in the midnight prayer.

II.

The white-robed choir moves along,
   And the solemn Mass is said,
The roof resounds with dirge and song
   For the soul of the recent dead ;

And incense burns, and tapers blaze
   Round altar and sculptured urn;—
Oh, for the fine old pious days!
   When will they again return?—
And the monk and the hermit leave their cells
At the sound of the old monastic bells!

III.

And these the men and these the times
   That a bigot age would brand
With all the guilt, and fraud, and crimes
   Which have since flowed o'er the land.
'Twas here the wretched wanderer found
   A home and a resting-place,
Young science threw its light around
   Each bower of prayer and peace,
Till royal rapine, with merciless hand,
Unsheathed the persecuting brand.[82]

IV.

And tyrants rose, and victims bled,
   And ruin and discord reigned,
Religion wildly shrieking fled
   From altar and shrine profaned!
Thrones, sceptres, crowns were swept away
   Like heath on a wintry wild:—
How much unlike that glorious day,
   When peace and content smiled,
And lake and valley re-echoed the knell
That came from the fine old monastic bell!

V.

Time brings a change, as years on years
    Roll on to the mighty past,
A star from out the gloom appears,
    And beams on the land at last.
Faith, Hope, and Charity return
    To the dear old classic shades,
And tapers and sweet incense burn
    Through aisles and long arcades ;
And now once more the breezes swell
With the dear old notes of the vesper bell !

Labourers' Lays.

No. 1.
I'VE HEARD THERE'S A STRANGER.

I.

I've heard there's a stranger come over to inspect us,[33]
   And prate of our poverty, patience, and parts,
With a scratch of a pen he would straightway direct us,
   And make every *gorsoon* a Master of Arts!

II.

He'll show us the way to gain *crockfuls* of riches,
   As sure as was e'er dug from haunted churchyard,
Use bone-dust, guano, pull down those cursèd ditches,
   And one day or other you'll have your reward.

III.

Fill up those old *gripes*, and keep constantly *draining*,
   Lay out all the money you ever can scrape;
When the rent comes around, never mind the distraining,
   You've sown, and, assuredly, *someone* will reap

IV.

Sow clover, and turnips, and vetches, and mangel,
　If you still have escaped from the kind auctioneer;
But if you then find you can no longer *wrangle*,
　Why, *give it all up*, and you've nothing to fear.

V.

You then may remove with your stool, *boss*, and table,
　Your pots and your kettles, your pot-hooks and pans,
And creep to the shelter of pig-cot or stable,
　Where nought shall prevent you to think of my plans.

VI.

And then you can pour over Smith's "Wealth of Nations,"
　With botany, chemistry, science *galore*,
And the deuce is then in it if, free from vexations,
　You're not better off than you e'er were before!

VII.

And thus with *big talk* they would try to persuade us
　To change our old plans, that 'twas all for our good,
But to let every pert English coxcomb degrade us
　Is what in Old Erin was ne'er understood!

No. 2.
THE "TIMES'" COMMISSIONER.*

"It is a singular fact that the farther you travel westward in Ireland the more beautiful does Nature appear to have been in heaping upon the country natural resources, and the less has been done by the hand of man to use and improve them. I speak advisedly when I say there is no part of England which possesses one-tenth of the means of creating wealth and prosperity which are to be found in this very county, Mayo, which in the best of times exhibits a degree of degraded wretchedness, such as will be in vain sought for in any part of England.—*The* "*Times*" *Commissioner.*

I.

YES, *Saxon*, GOD had made us
    The fairest isle that lights the waves,
Till *man* sought to degrade us,
    And make us abject, willing slaves.
They could not, though they wasted
    With fire and sword our fertile plains,
The soul that once hath tasted
    Bright freedom, ne'er can rest in chains.

II.

For centuries they drove us
    To deep morass and mountain glen;
And though they seem to love us,
    They'd dare the demon deed again,

---

* The *Times'* Commissioner sent over to Ireland to report on the agricultural prospects and general condition of the country.

Did they not feel the spirit
  That proudly spurns the despot's sway;
Though poor, we still inherit
  The daring of a brighter day.

III.

Where'er their steps polluted
  One wide-spread ruin strewed the ground,
Lov'd homes and fanes uprooted,
  And all made one wild desert round.
But now, they kindly send us
  A hireling scribe to mock our pain:[34]
From all such God defend us,
  They never can succeed again.

No. 3.

THE HOMES OF IRELAND.

I.

THE fine old homes of Ireland,
  How silently they stand,
Amid the ruin and decay
  Of this ill-fated land!

The nettle grows upon the hearth,
    The long grass in the hall;
Instead of music, song, and mirth,
    A deep gloom covers all.

II.

The abbey homes of Ireland,
    Where saints and sages dwelt,
The altars and the village church,
    Where our forefathers knelt,
No more with vesper songs resound,
    Nor matin's sacred hymn,
Their fragments strew the holy ground,
    All there is dark and dim.

III.

The cabin homes of Ireland!
    Around their hearths by night,
What looks of wretched poverty
    Meet round the cheerless light!
The mother's voice is heard to sing
    Her starving babes to sleep;
The father can no comfort bring,
    He can but watch and weep.

IV.

The squalid homes of Ireland!
    How long will they remain?
As long as native millions bow
    And kiss the tyrant's chain!

Until the councils of the brave
Unite us one and all—
Then, freedom shall beam round the slave,
And smile in hut and hall.

No. 4.

IS THERE A HEART IN ERIN'S ISLE.

I.

Is there a heart in Erin's Isle,
   Whate'er its caste or creed may be,
So cold and callous, base and vile,
   As not to wish its country free?
Is not our land supremely fair,
   Our own green Eden of the west?
Then why should discord taint the air,
   And strive to lacerate her breast?

II.

Her glorious smile beams bright on all,
   No matter at what shrine we kneel;
The peasant's hut, the princely hall,
   Must ever share her woe or weal.
Oh! then, why will a wretched pride,
   A foolish colour turn astray
Some souls that should be on the side
   Of justice and our rights to-day?

No. 5.

SONG OF THE PEOPLE.

"Let no man despise the secret hints and motives of danger which sometimes are given to him, when he may think there is no probability of its being real."—DE FOE.

I.

THE earth, the beauteous earth, was made,
With swelling hill and spreading glade,
For man to till the grateful soil,
And live by sweet, industrious toil.

II.

The land with every changing scene,
The prairies wild, the valleys green,
And the unfathomed, boundless sea
Were made for man, great God, by Thee!

III.

He meted out the sun's broad ray,
The dewdrop on the tiny spray,
And pour'd with an unsparing hand
Abundance o'er the teeming land.

IV.

No fence, no clime, no zone confines
The air, the dew, the sun that shines:
Then why should sacrilegious hands
Be laid on God's—the people's lands?

V.

The bird that flies from tree to tree,
The beast that roams the wild is free;
Then why should man for ever toil
An outcast on his native soil?

No 6.

THE SONG OF THE IRISH ARTIZAN.

I.

THERE are treasures deep hid
   In the depths of thy fountains,
And marble, and gold, too,
   Concealed in thy mountains;
And, oh! how enchanting
   While we wander along
To listen by moonlight
   To the corn-reapers' song:
      Erin, dear Erin!

II.

There are riches untold
    And untouched scattered round thee,
But the chain of the vampire
    Too tightly has bound thee;
Till the blood of thy bravest
    Flow'd in waste, like thy waters,
And thy soil was made fat
    With the burning and slaughters:
        Erin, dear Erin!

III.

The curse of the stranger
    Is still hanging o'er thee,
And crushes the prospects
    Of those who adore thee:
Like the tempest that shatters
    The eagle's lone dwelling,
And blights those high hopes
    That in strong hearts are swelling:
        Erin, dear Erin!

IV.

The home of the Celt is
    Now lonely and cheerless,
And the spirit once light
    And once buoyant and fearless

Is pining away
  In his lov'd land of sorrow
With scarce one ray of hope
  To enliven the morrow:
    Erin, dear Erin!

v.

The peasants that delved
  In both valley and highland
Are flying like geese
  From their own holy island;
And those who remain
  Are like foes, disunited;—
Oh, sure, 'tis no wonder
  That thou are benighted,
    Erin, dear Erin!

No. 7.

DEAR LAND.

I.

DEAR land! dear blighted, ruined land,
  Though clouds and darkness spread
Their funeral pall from strand to strand
  Above thy martyred dead,

Though thou art now one vast churchyard,
    A charnel-house of gloom,
Still there are who keep watch and ward
    Above the nation-tomb!

II.

Dear land! dear patient, suffering land,
    Though false and foolish knaves
Would bid thee draw thy glittering brand
    And be their willing slaves,
Yet in thy worst and weakest hour,
    Thy spirit still retains
Too much of native pride and power
    To kiss those flowery chains.

III.

Dear land! dear land! I love thee still,
    My own bright, blessed isle;
There's holy light upon each hill
    And hope in thy sweet smile,
Which shone through darkness, blood, and tears,
    And burns bright to-day—
The birthright of a thousand years,
    Which never will decay.

No. 8.
A BALLAD OF THE YEAR 1849, THE YEAR OF FAMINE.

" —While children cry and call for bread,
  And cry and call in vain,
Th' unconscious parent, cold and dead;
  Alas!—by famine slain!"
                    JUVERNICUS.

I.

THE mist was falling thick and fast
  Upon the sloe-thorn glen,
The brook brawled hoarsely as it past
  The wild and willowy fen;
The night wind whistled sharp and shrill
  Along the copse-wood side,
The moon climbed up her silent hill
  In cold and cheerless pride.

II.

Dark, dreary, indistinct, and lone,
  An old gray ruin stands—
The moss is on the altar-stone,
  The bell in other lands: [36]
No statue, painting, priest is there,
  No voice is raised to bless;
And yet one form bends in prayer
  Amid that loneliness.

III.

A fair young peasant girl, the pride
    Of all the country round,
In that lone hour kneels beside
    A new-made grassy mound,
Like some sad ghost that lingers where
    Its buried treasures lie,
And nightly guards them still with care
    From every mortal eye.[37]

IV.

The silent stars look down upon
    The orphan daughter's tears:
Oh! well may weep the lonely one
    Beneath their cold, pale spheres;
For Hope's own blessed beams which fed
    That soul have passed away,
And all she ever loved are dead
    And turning into clay.

V.

A mother's voice no more can bring
    Fresh lustre to thy brow,
No more thou'lt hear that voice, poor thing,
    Thou hast no mother now!
Nor father, for the famine came,
    And fever's burning breath
Soon, soon consigned that dear lov'd name
    To solitude and death.

VI.

And thou art left, the only one
    Of all whose smiles have made
A paradise within the home
    Round which thy childhood played ;—
But no ! the living spring has failed,
    The caskets, spoiled and riven ;
The soul like morning dew exhaled,
    And flew to its bright heaven !

National Melodies.

No. 1.

MEN OF WEXFORD.

I.

Men of Wexford, halt not, pause not,
   While you still have work to do;
Wipe away that burning plague spot
   That too long has hung o'er you.
'Twas your shores were first invaded
   By a foreign Saxon band,
Wexford slept not then, nor dreaded
   To attack them on the strand.[38]

II.

'Twas our sires first bled for freedom,
   'Twas their blood was last to flow;
And should e'er our country need them,
   We have hearts to face the foe.

Though they poured their blood like water
    Free on many a hard-fought plain,
All this carnage, gore, and slaughter
    But cemented Erin's chain.

III.

In the time of every danger
    Wexford took a noble part:
Can the bonds of slavery change her,
    Will she show a craven's heart?
No, by every link that binds us
    To the bright but bloody past,
Erin still shall ever find us
    " Slow but sure " to win at last.[39]

IV.

Let the past direct and guide us,
    Let the present ever show
That no change can e'er divide us
    Practised by the wily foe.
Then once more let Wexford rally,
    And keep up the bloodless fight;
Let each mountain, rock, and valley
    Ring with—" Persevere! unite!"

No. 2.

BRIGHT, BRIGHT WAS THE MORN.

(*A Song of the Shielmaliers.*)

I.

Bright, bright was the morn when the bold shielmalier,
Undaunted by bayonet, a stranger to fear,
Sprang up from his heather-couch, sparkling with dew,
To muster with Grogan, Hay, Harvey and Keogh !
He paused not to take a last look at his cot,
Or the loved ones that clung to that favourite spot ;
Yet a tear dimmed his eye, as he bounded along,
When he heard through the copse-wood his Mary's sweet song.

II.

Ay, listen again to that soft, plaintive voice,
'Tis the last thou wilt hear from the maid of thy choice.
One moment he faltered, and yet he was brave :—
" My country her freedom, or freemen a grave !
Let the craven and coward inactive remain,
And bless the oppressor while forging his chain ;
But never again shall we seek our repose
Till our banners triumphantly float o'er our foes ! "

III.

The green flags are streaming from hill-top and glen,
The valleys resound with the trampling of men,
And woodland and mountain are bristling with spears
Of thousands of dauntless and bold shielmaliers!
Like torrents resistless they rush on the foe,
And horses and riders at once are laid low,
And helmets and halberts are shivered in twain,
And plumed caps and colours are strewed on the plain!

IV.

Oh! where are the thousands in glittering array
That swept o'er the field at the dawning of day?
Their chivalry's faded, their glory is past,
Their trumpets no more shall be heard on the blast!
They came in the pride and the trappings of war,
But their legions were broken and scattered afar,
Not a vestige remains, not a banner is seen,
Save the standard of Erin—the bright, fadeless green!

V.

The foe fled like cowards, but ruin marked their flight,
And chapels and cottages blazed through the night;

And the shouts of the spoilers were heard on the gale,
Commingling with woman's deep, heartrending wail.
But vows of wild vengeance rose madly beside
The death-bed of many a maniac bride:
Men swore, as beside their ruined altars they stood,
That they'd wash out the stain of defilement by blood.

VI.

Let Oulart, and Arklow, and Ross truly tell
How the cohorts of Britain ingloriously fell.
A voice from the past cries, in warning, " Beware
Of what the infuriate peasant will dare!"[40]
Oh, never again let wild war's bloody hand
Be raised 'gainst the freedom and faith of our land!
Oh, never again let the red flag and green
In hostile array in our country be seen!

No. 3.

OH! BLAME NOT THE MEN.

I.

OH! blame not the men who for liberty perished,
 The fearless in heart who devotedly bled!
Long, long shall their memory through Erin be cherished,
 Long, long shall we mourn o'er the shrines of the dead!

They are gone, but around them a light is still
　　burning,
　　Like a sentinel star o'er young Liberty's sleep,
And when from their tombs the bold peasant's
　　returning,
　　His vows rise for freedom, low, noiseless, but
　　　deep!

II.

In vain did the cold-hearted Saxon endeavour
　　To darken those deeds on our history's page,
For ages of bondage and suffering shall never
　　Erase one lov'd name from that chivalrous
　　　age.
No; as well might they stem the pure feeling still
　　gushing
　　O'er hearts and o'er harp-strings, by mountain and
　　　sea,
As restrain that high patriot-spirit that's rushing
　　In might over millions resolved to be free.

III.

They failed where great Washington purchased his
　　glory,
　　But their motives, their feelings, their lives were
　　　the same,
And though they have fallen, in Erin's proud
　　story,
　　Free Liberty's light shall emblazon each name!

Long, long shall we chant, to the wild strain undying,
  The deeds of the dauntless, the bold, and the free,
Who, on to the last the fell Saxon defying,
  Were true on the scaffold, dear Erin, to thee!

No. 4.

BY SLANEY'S BANKS.

I.

By Slaney's banks I love to roam
  When moonbeams calmly sleep,
And every star in heaven above
  Is mirrored in the deep:
I love to view by that soft light
  Glen, cliff, and winding strand,
The keep where first a foreign knight
  Insulted our bright land.

II.

There lone, and dark, and silently
  It frowns above the waves,
The tomb of our lost liberty,
  Where freemen knelt as slaves.
There stands the record of our shame,
  Our country's first disgrace,
A blot upon her ancient name,
  Which time can ne'er efface.

III.

Though Erin never more may see
    Her *sunburst* proudly borne,
With *banners* of her *tanistry*,
    Upon the breeze of morn;
And though that age has passed away,
    Its spirit still remains,
And pours its bright, refulgent ray
    O'er Erin's lovely plains.

IV.

Then let her sons once more unite,
    And catch the sacred flame,
Till with a nation's power and might
    She wins a nation's name!
Thus like the solar beams which blend
    All colours into one
Shall Irishmen unite as friends,
    And then—their work is done!

No. 5.

SING ME THAT LITTLE SONG AGAIN.

I.

Sing me that little song again
    You used to sing to me
At home in holy Ireland,
    Beneath our spreading tree;

The lonely stream, the hazel dells,
  The children all at play,
Rise up before me when you sing
  The same as on that day.

II.

Oh! how I wish once more to roam
  Beside the old spring well,
Where last I met the neighbours all,
  To say my last farewell;
But this, alas! can never be,
  Except when mem'ry strays
Like day-dreams to those happy times,
  The scenes of former days.

No. 6.

THE WISH.

I.

THOUGH poor, I ask not riches now,
  Nor ought that wealth bestows;
A nobler thought is on my brow,
  And in my bosom glows.

II.

I ask not throne or diadem,
  Supported by the slave;
A brighter, richer, purer gem,
  Is in the boon I crave.

III.

I seek not Love's soft scenes of bliss,
   Nor beauty's brilliant smile;
A scene more exquisite than this
   Must this fond heart beguile.

IV.

I care not for the conqueror's fame,
   When prostrate nations kneel;
A far more strong and holier flame
   Excites my warmest zeal.

V.

The voice that cheers the child of song,
   Though sweet its praise may be,
Still, still a wish, more sweet, more strong,
   More exquisite for me.

VI.

Of all the magic gifts that make
   A fairy's treasury,
Oh! give me that which quickest brake
   Our chains, and set us free!

No. 7.

SONG.

The whole *slave may be kept stationary, the* half *slave never!"*—THE ANGLO-IRISH OF THE NINETEENTH CENTURY.

Go, tell the bold Briton, in triumph and pride,
He never again can corrupt or divide
The hearts that are pledged, and the souls that are brave,
Who wipes from each brow the foul blot of the slave,
And shook off those chains which no more shall disgrace
Our country, religion, our name, and our race.

II.

Too oft we have poured out the national song,
In useless regret, o'er our country's wrong,
Unheeded we've wept o'er each link of the chain.
And knelt to the Saxon, and prayed, but in vain:
Unpitied they saw all our greatness decay,
Like some desolate ruin whose master's away.

III.

At last the proud spirit of Erin arose,
And flashed out the lightning of thought on her foes;

O'er mountain and valley resistless it darts,
And lights up the long-treasured hope of our hearts,
That burned for ages like fires that glow
Unseen in the depths of the mountains below.

IV.

The spirit, oft broken by faction and strife,
Now rises refreshed with new vigour and life;
No tyrant can weaken, no fetters can bind
The force that lies shrined in the depths of the mind;
No dastard can mar, and no traitor can blight
The full blaze of freedom when millions unite!

No. 8.

"We are the successors of the martyrs, and we do not tremble before the successors of Julian the Apostate. We are the sons of the crusaders, and we will not retreat before the offspring of Voltaire."—COUNT DE MONTALEMBERT.

I.

CAN the Church of God be blighted?
  Will our Prelates now give way
To that *ignis fatuus*, lighted
  But to dazzle and betray?
No! we vow, by shrines uprooted,
  By the altars of our land,
Never shall they be polluted
  By the sceptic's daring hand.

II.

True, the sword no more is gleaming
    O'er us, as in days of yore,
Nor the votary's life-blood streaming
    On the consecrated floor:
These were tried, but each endeavour
    Served but closer still to bind
Hearts that nought on earth could sever
    From their God and from mankind.

III.

Shall we quench the lights that guide us,
    Now as in a former day;
Can the subtle arts divide us
    Of an enemy at bay?
Never!—Let the deep recesses,
    Where our fathers bent the knee,
Find a tongue, while each expresses
    " Never!—never!—altars free!"

No. 9.

THE ENGLISH POOR-HOUSE.

I.

An old man stood at the Poor-house gate,
    And begged for bread and board;
But the surely porter turned away,
    For none would he afford.

The stars blazed out in the frosty sky,
   The earth was white with snow;
God pity the poor forsaken one,
   He knows not where to go.

II.

He is far away from his native vale,
   That rises bright and fair,
Like a paradise o'er Memory's sight,
   To heighten his despair.
Again does his humble cottage home
   And blazing hearth appear,
And kind old friends of his youth once more
   Stand round to soothe and cheer.

III.

Ah! 'tis but a dream, from which he turns
   In bitterness of grief:
An outcast he, by the bleak hill-side,
   Meets with but small relief.
They call him a stranger, though he gave
   His youth and strength of years
To the selfish Briton who now mocks
   His feebleness and tears.

IV.

An alien!—how could he dare to hope
   For aid in his hour of need
From the bigot stranger who detests
   His country and his creed?

Poor, friendless, old, deserted now,
  They drive him from their shore;
Go, starve in thy boasted fertile land,
  But taint our shore no more.

v.

And thus he's cast, like a withered weed,
  A wreck upon the strand,
A stranger without health, hope, or home,
  Upon his native land.
Few, few the wants of the wretched man,
  And yet the exiled slave
Was driven to what was once his home
  To find in it the grave!

No. 10.

SONG.

BRING BACK, BRING BACK.

I.

BRING back, bring back those golden hours,
  Ere trials could impart
A shade to dim the soul's bright flowers,
  The sabbath of the heart.

II.

Oh! bring them back, if but to tell
  How cold and changed we're now,
And fling the magic of their spell
  Once more upon this brow,

No II.

OH! ERIN OF THE MOUNTAINS.

I.

OH! Erin of the mountains,
  Of glowing glens and sun-lit lakes,
Of fairy-haunted fountains,
  Of fertile glades and tangled brakes;
The "light from heaven," that led thee
  So safely over perils past,
Will make each tyrant dread thee,
  And crown thy brightest hopes at last.

II.

Thou art too pure and peerless,
  Too powerful to be held in thrall;
Thy sons are firm and fearless
  In battle's blaze and peaceful hall:

And oh, thy daughters' glances
  And smiles are given in witchery
To him who most advances
  The glorious cause of liberty.

III.

Then who would shrink or falter
  Before the Saxon's smile or frown ?—
Oh ! never shall they alter
  Our fixed resolve or put it down.
With the bright sky above us,
  And Erin's flowery vales below,
With smiles from those who love us,
  Oh, who would quail before the foe !

No. 12.

TO A MOUNTAIN FERN.

I.

CHILD of the eagle's rocky eyrie,
Of lonely rath and glen of fairy,
Where the wild roe, faint and weary,
      Oft found rest ;
Where the mountain winds are sighing,
Where the timid hare is lying,
And the stock-dove softly crying
      Round its nest !

II.

Far away where streams are springing,
Where the blackbird's notes are ringing
Through the hawthorn shade that's flinging
    Perfume round,
Or beside the haunted cairn,
'Midst the wildest scenes of Erin,
There, romantic mountain fern,
    Thou art found.

III.

Hermit of the lonely places,
Where nor men nor time effaces
Those old Ossianic traces,
    Which still last,
Like the voice of former ages,
Coming from our bards and sages,
Through the dim but glorious ages
    Of the past!

IV.

Thou hast seen *Fionn's* banners streaming,
And his shields and lances beaming,
Like blue meteors wildly gleaming
    Through the air;
And where rock and caverned valley
Sounded with the gathering rally:
    "Thou wert there."

V.

Ah, but since those deeds of glory,
Blazoned forth in song and story,
Wounded, hunted down, and gory,
  The poor kern
Often sought thy green recesses,
Where his bleeding bosom presses
Thy cool leaf, then dying blesses
  Erin, still Erin!

No. 13.

O KATHLIN! SING THAT SONG AGAIN.

I

O KATHLIN! sing that song again,
 For it brings back to me
The perfume of my native glen
 And the old favourite tree,
Beneath whose shade I heard it first,
 Ere time had swept away
Those day-dreams which I fondly nursed
 In life's young ardent day.

II.

I feel again the free, fresh air
 Of the fields upon my brow,
And in despite of years of care
 I'm almost happy now.

The woodbine's living fragrance dwells
   Within each simple strain,
And wakes from Memory's thousand cells
   Bright dreams of youth again!

No. 14.

WAKE! ERIN, WAKE!

I.

WAKE! Erin, wake! freemen and slaves,
   Awake! arise to do your duty;
Pledged by your martyred heroes' graves
   To live for country, home, and beauty,
      Beauty! beauty!
Pledged by your martyred heroes' graves
   To live for country, home, and beauty,

II.

Too long thou'st slept, or only woke
   To rush tumultuously to danger;
And then thy deadliest vengeance broke
   Upon the proud, imperious stranger,
      Stranger! stranger!
And then thy deadliest vengeance broke
   Upon the proud, imperious stranger.

III.

The short lived triumph soon was past,
   And then thy golden prospects faded,
Home, lov'd ones, life were on the cast,
   And all were ruined or degraded,
        Degraded! degraded!
Home, lov'd ones, life were on the cast,
   And all were ruined or degraded.

IV.

Yes, wake! but not with flashing brand,
   With trumpets' clang and banners flying,
On gore-stained fields to take your stand,
   And charge o'er neighbours, dead and dying,
        Dying! dying!
On gore-stained fields to take your stand,
   And charge o'er neighbours dead and dying.

V.

No; 'tis your greatest son that waves
   The olive branch o'er sect and station,
And cries: "Oh, be for ever slaves,
   Or join with me and be a nation!
        Nation! nation!"
And cries: "Oh, be for ever slaves,
   Or join with me and *be a nation!*"[41]

No 15.

THE SUMMER IS COME BACK AGAIN.

I.

The summer is come back again,
  To leaf, and flower, and tree;
The birds are singing in the glen,
  The streams leap bright with glee;
But summer's beams, or summer's flowers,
  Alas! cannot renew
The chieftains of those fine old times,
  The Dane and Saxon slew.

II.

The glens, the glades are little changed,
  Our mountains are as grand
As when our princes o'er them ranged
  The monarchs of our land.
But, oh! the slavery of years
  Has dimmed the nation's brow,
O'Donnell's, Sarsfield's, Edward's spears—
  Where are those heroes now?

III.

O'Donnell sleeps in foreign clay,[42]
  Sarsfield on Landen fell;[43]
Lord Edward's spirit passed away
  In Newgate's dungeon cell.[44]

Oh, then the nation's heart was rent,
    Her banners sunk in gore,
She stood a rifled monument,
    Her nation-voice was o'er.

IV.

Yet freedom's spirit never dies,
    But like a secret spring,
Whose waters in the desert rise,
    Fresh, clear, and bright of wing;
And 'midst the lifeless, arid sands,
    Spreads vegetation round,
So her bright spirit, too, expands,
    Above the heroes' mound.

V.

Yes, while one worshipper remains
    Beside our ivied shrines,
There also, amid broken chains,
    The light of freedom shines!
And though the deadly "Crom-a-boo"
    And pibrock's clang is past,
The millions are to Erin true,
    And love her to the last.

No. 16.

TO MARY O'DONNELL,*

In reply to her Song of Invitation to Tyrconnell.

I

Sad is thy tale, poor maid of the woody-wild,
   Dead are thy warrior-chiefs of Tyrconnell,
Silent the halls where valiant *Cuchullin* smiled,
   Yet sweet is the harp of our *Mary O'Donnell!*
      There to the pale moonbeams,
      Down by thy winding streams,
Thoughts of the past o'er thy music are stealing,
      Deep as the sighs that start
      Fresh from the wounded heart,
All the rich gems of thy pure soul revealing.

II.

Bright are the deeds of thy fathers in story,
   High on the list was bold *Ullin* in fame,
Glittering round with a halo of glory,
   Far flashed their vengeance in terror and flame!
      But of that glorious day
      All has now passed away,

---

* Mary O'Donnell was the assumed name of one of the song-writers of the *Wexford Independent*;

Save the high spirit that lives in thy numbers;
   Oh ! let it wake the slave,
   Standing on Freedom's grave,
Once more to rise from his lethargic slumbers.

III.

Old Wexford was first 'gainst the freeman to rally,
   And met the invader with *hackbut* and *brand*,
Lost freedom's last battle-cry rang through our valley,
   The last of the free were the men of our land.
      Some of them fighting fell
      Guarding their native dell,
Others now rest in the land of the stranger:
      Green shall their memory be,
      Held by the bold and free,
Patriot spirits who blenched not at danger.

IV.

While memories like these brightly round us are shining,
   With strains from thy harp to inspire and to cheer;
Oh ! where is the Helot for liberty pining,
   Would halt in his powerful and glorious career;
      And while one link remains,
      Cormac's, MacOssian's strains,[45]

Ever shall mingle with those of Tyrconnell;
    And could I hope to be
      Blessed with one smile from thee,
Gladly I'd fly to thee, Mary O'Donnell!

No. 17.

THE IRISH MOTHER'S LAMENT TO HER SON WHO HAD ENLISTED.

(Inscribed with sincere respect to Shemus Ullina.)

I.

O SHEMUS! O Shemus! you're my heart's delight!
Why did you enlist with the Saxon to fight?
Oh! little I thought, when you played at my knee,
That I'd see this black day, my own Cushla-ma-chree.

II.

I never could bear since the year ninety-eight
The sight of a red-coat; for, early or late,[46]
Wherever they went, they spread terror around:
Oh! such villains, I'm sure, ne'er walked Irish ground.

III.

Though the food it was scanty, and you were ill paid,
My darling, 'twas better than to wear the cockade;
For what's all their glory, their triumphs, and wars
To the poor Irish soldier, with nothing but scars?

IV.

They tear you from home and from friends you love well,
From the fields where you played in your own native dell,
To pour out your heart's blood in war's deadly strife,
In some far distant land, my sole joy and my life!

V.

Then where will you turn, some comfort to fin d
The foe is before you, there's terror behind:
No chapel, no altar, no *soggarth* is there,
But tumult, and curses, and groans fill the air.

VI.

God pity me, Shemus! *alanna*, good-bye!
My grief is too heavy and deep now to cry;
My poor heart is breaking—I'll soon be laid low,
My blessing be with you wherever you go!

No. 18.

THE EMIGRANT'S FAREWELL.

Gratefully and affectionately dedicated to Cormac Ulla.

I.

OH! God be with thee, Ireland!
Thou lov'd land of my birth!
Farewell ye mountains wild and grand,
Scenes of my childhood's mirth,

The broad, blue billows soon shall roll
  Between me and thy strand,
But still the exile's heart and soul
  Shall turn to fatherland.

II.

Yes, yes, I've learned to love thy name
  Beside my father's knee,
While listening with a soul on flame
  To thy soft minstrelsy:
There many a long, long winter's night,
  Around the bogwood's blaze,
Legend of mountain, glen, and sprite
  Was told of other days.

III.

Old Owen would in raptures tell
  Of sparry halls of light,
Where warriors rest by magic spell,
  Accoutred for the fight;
Or of some fairy's shining home
  Beneath a rath or cairn
Where sweet, wild music seems to come
  From some old withered fern.

IV.

And then with wild and flashing eye,
  He'd seize a burning brand,
And fiercely shout some battle cry,
  Or war-note of our land,

Or tell how valliant OWEN ROE
Swept mountain-pass and vale
Of every trace of foreign foe
And craven of the Pale.

V.

But, ah! those pleasant days are past
And can return no more;
E'en now the dreary winter's blast
Sweeps o'er the cottage floor.
The "agent" came one wintery day,
The snow was on the ground;
He ordered us like beasts away
To make a desert round.

VI.

What, though the Ohio's banks are fair
And Maine and Vermont free,
I still shall be an exile there,
My *home* beyond the sea.
Farewell! already from my view
Recedes the lessening strand;
But this fond heart and soul so true
Shall turn to fatherland.

No. 19.

AWAKE, YE BARDS.

To Cormac Ulla.

I.

Lov'D brother bard of the " single string,"
Of the soul of flame and the heart of a king,
Of deep-toned songs that with them bring
      High hopes and purpose strong;
You call once more on the bards to tell
By what banshee, thorn, or fairy-well
They have passed, since some unearthly spell
      Seems to quench the light of song.

II.

I have wandered by the Owenvarra's wave,
But all is silent there as the grave;
I have passed the spot where sleep the brave
      By Tara's mouldering fanes;
I have lately stood where legends say
The giant sleeps in his shroud of clay,[47]
But both bard and harp were far away,
      And hushed their glorious strains.

III.

I sought for a cause in heaven's blue height,
But all was beautiful there and bright,
The stars of GOD decked the robes of night,
      And the moon shone full and fair

As when she lighted the Hebrew race
To a free and fruitful dwelling-place ;
And not a sign in heaven could I trace,
    No cause for a change was there.

IV.

And I turned again to the beauteous earth—
But, oh, what a change in the peasant's heart!
The laughing eye and the song of mirth
    Were changed to wailings deep ;
For Famine had stalked o'er each fertile spot,
O'er the lordly hall, and the poor man's cot.
Oh, God help the poor, for man does not,
    But consigns them to death's cold sleep.

V.

Oh! can it be that the sons of song
Have no voice to lash this monstrous wrong ?
Awake, ye bards!—ye have slept too long,
    For Cormac Ulla calls!
For me—both in dark and sunny hour,
While my voice has strength and my harp has
    power—
I shall strike its strings in my rustic bower
    Till proud oppression falls!

No. 20.

THE OLD CHURCHYARD.

I.

An aged man, with silvery hair and careworn face, was seen
In a neglected old churchyard, and he stood by a knoll of green;
And he looked up to the smiling sky, and he looked o'er the sea,
And, sighing, said, as he raised his head: "There's no home or hope for me!"

II.

The old whitethorns bloomed around, and the grass was rank and long,
And from the hazel wood came forth the blackbird's mellow song,
And the doves cooed on the elm boughs, and the osier kissed the stream,
And the sun o'er all threw his golden pall as he shed his evening beam.

III.

But he heeded not the tranquil scene, nor minded sun or flower—
One thought alone sunk on his heart in that distressing hour—

Beneath the green sod's silent breast lay every hope and joy:
His darling son, now dead and gone, his dark-haired, whitefoot boy!

IV.

"They called him murderer," he said, " because he loved his home,
Because he could not bear to see his aged father roam
A houseless outcast of the wild, no place to lay his head
When the wintery blast blew cold and fast around his thorny shed.

V.

"And when he heard his mother moan and saw his sister cry,
Deep-seated vengeance filled his heart and frenzy lit his eye;
The rich man heeded not our woe nor cared for our distress,
But very soon the broad, bright moon looked on one tyrant less!

VI.

"The fearful deed was promptly done; but, oh! the crime, the guilt—
Oh! was it not upon the head of him whose blood was spilt?

'Twas he that raised the demon up that did himself destroy,
And with him died my heart's sole pride—my murdered white-foot boy!

VII.

" Oh, when will mankind learn to feel that we have sympathies,
And kindly feelings, too, till nipt by cold misfortune's breeze;
Oh, could they know the poor man's wrongs, his sufferings and distress,
A nation's might would then unite to bring us quick redress.

VIII.

" For me, my race is nearly run, each thing I loved is gone,
And, like some blasted tree, I'm left to wither here alone.
I only ask a resting-place beneath yon big white-thorn,
Secure at last from winter's blast and man's malignant scorn!"

NATIONAL MELODIES.

No. 21.
SING ON, SING ON.

I.

Sing on, sing on, that blessed strain
   I've heard in happier times than this;
Yet stay, repeat it not again,
   'Twill 'waken memory into bliss.

II.

Sing on, sing on, I'll learn to bear
   That voice, that tone so like the same
I used long, long ago to hear,
   So soft, so sweet the music came.

III.

Sing on, sing on, though this heart break,
   I cannot lose those of heaven,
Now blending all that can awake
   The past with present sweetness given!

No. 22.
THE FETCH.

I.

I knew he'd die!
For the moon's sweet ray
Shone as bright as day,

And meteors red
    Flashed through the sky
As some spirit fled
    From its home on high,
To play 'mid bowers
Of moonlight flowers,
Until morning came
With its slanting beam,
When he'd soar away
To the new-born day.

II.

I knew he'd die!
For the Banshee's song
All the whole night long
Was heard from the bawn,
    And its wailing cry
Only ceased with the dawn;
    Then the owl flew by
With its mournful scream
From the early beam,
And the measured stroke
Of the death-watch spoke
Weak, but sadly clear
To the sick man's ear.

III.

I knew he'd die!
For the *Fetch* was seen
In the green boreen

By the fairy's path;
    And no one came by
The old haunted rath
    When eve's starlight eye
Look down on the earth
With its flowers and mirth,
But heard wildly rung
From some spirit's tongue
His name—and I knew
That his days were few!

No. 23.

LISTEN TO THE FAIRIES SINGING.

I.

LISTEN to the fairies singing
    Yonder in the rath;
Oh, how sweet their notes are ringing
    Down the haunted path.

II.

Do you hear soft voices calling
    Someone far away,
While the midnight dews are falling
    On the elfin spray.

III.

'Round us everywhere there's wailing :
    'Tis no place to be;
Spirits through the night are sailing,
    Though we cannot see.

IV.

In the hazel glen there's sighing
    On the moonlight air;
'Tis the Fallen Angels crying,
    Crying out their prayer.

No. 24.

THE BANSHEE'S SONG.

I.

COME away, the morn is breaking,
    Come away before 'tis day,
Nothing here is worth thy taking,
    Come away, come away!
Why should there be weeping, wailing,
    Why should there be sighs and tears?
Come away! they're unavailing,
    Come to heaven's happy spheres!

II.

Come away, the moonlight's sleeping
    Brightly on each flower and spray,
'Tis the spirits' hour for keeping
    Watch before the break of day.

Voices on the air are speaking,
    Come! be not afraid to die;
Night is past, the dawn is breaking,
    The bright vales of heaven are nigh!

III.

Come away, thy angel's bringing
    Spirits bright to guard thy way,
Listen, don't you hear them singing
    In the clouds up far away?
They will lead thee to bright bowers
    Where the lov'd ones ever pray;
Why delay those glorious hours?
    Sister spirit, come away.

No. 25.

TO ERIN.

LET me weave a chaplet now,
Erin, for thy glorious brow,
Cull them from the ruined shrine
Where the ivy tendrils twine;
From the long-deserted hall,
Pluck them from the ruined wall,
Gather every flower that grew
In the midnight moonlight dew;
From the graves of that bright band
Who died for love of fatherland;

Everyone that o'er us cast
Visions of the painful past,
And engraves upon the heart
What thou *wert* and what thou *art!*
Erin!, fairest spot on earth,
Oh! remember what thou wert,
Ere the Norman stranger came
To malign thy sainted name,
And with bloody spear and brand
To enslave our lovely land;
Or, with false, delusive smile,
Plunder our confiding isle;
Since Fitzstephen came to aid
The licentious renegade,
And with rude, marauding host
Landed on the Wexford coast,
And erected on the side
Of the Slaney's silver tide,
The first keep of Norman power,
Ferry Carrig's feudal tower;—
Oh! since the destruction tore
From each wounded, suffering pore
All those lov'd and holy things
From which a nation's greatness springs.
Thou hast seen thy princes kneel
While they kissed the tyrant's heel,
Reeking with the patriot blood
Of the dauntless few who stood
Firm and fast through weal or woe,
Who in death still aimed a blow

At the foremost foeman's head,
Or the crouching slave who fled.
Thou hast seen thy altars, where
Saints and sages knelt in prayer,
Blazing from the bigot's brand,
Crushed by the mad despot's hand;
Yet not altogether rent,
Though full many a monument,
Mouldering, desolate, and lone,
Speak of deeds that have been done—
Of the piety and crimes
Which belonged to other times.
Yes, my country, thou hast seen
All thy lovely glens of green,
Where the bard had loved to roam
By his peaceful, sylvan home,
Bristling with the foeman's spear,
Who, in red war's wild career,
Turned each flowery soft recess
Into one wild wilderness;
Trampled on their plighted faith,
Cruel, treacherous, ingrate!—
Severed all the links that bind
Men to country and mankind;
Plucked each radiant, peerless gem
From thy sparkling diadem,
Until, more audacious grown,
They struck down the ancient throne,

That for centuries had stood
Firm and fast through scenes of blood.
Oh! 'twas then thou felt'st the dart
Rankling in thy bleeding heart,
Trimmed with feathers from thy wing,
Which gave the most poignant sting.
Then they trampled on thy brow,
Pale and feeble, throneless now,
The deep brand of serf and slave,
Thou Eden of the western wave!
Oh! no more thy chieftains bear
Thy green banner high in air;
Oh! no more the axe and brand
Glitter in thy warrior's hand :
All is dark and dim despair—
Even hope scarce beaming there.
Yet, at length, one little star
In the distance burns afar :
Now another steady light—
One, two, three—now all is bright!
Giving light and warmth too,
Ever brilliant, steady, true,
Darting beams of brightness where
Nought e'er entered save despair,
Shedding lustre everywhere!
Then, my country, ne'er despair;
Meet, unite, and persevere;
Let thy watchward ever be
Peace and unanimity.

Rally round the olive wreath ;
Be firm, patient, not afraid ;
Place no confidence in those
Who have ever been thy foes ;
Do not believe the word that's wrung
Unwillingly from an " alien " tongue ;
They deceived thee once before,
Never, never trust them more.
'Tis not foreign influence mars
Thy fair promise, but the jars,
The disputes, and senseless rage
Which thy children ceaseless wage
With each other, like a brood
Of harpies quarrelling for food.
Oh, my country ! when shall cease
This disastrous disgrace ?
When shall all her sons be true
To each other and to you ?
When this comes, as come it will,
Light shall shine on every hill,
And a voice, loud, strong, and deep
Round our sea-girt isle shall sweep,
Sounding forth, with trumpet blast,
" Erin ! happy, free at last !"

No. 26.

STANZAS TO ERIN.

I.

My own green land, I loved thee since the time
I knew what 'twas to love, nor thought it crime
To worship aught so beautiful as thee,
For thou art lovely, and I thought thee free.

II.

Yes, thou art lovely—the same glorious smile
Is beaming still upon thy ocean isle,
That wooed so sweetly the young Geraldine,[48]
To arm for thee with princes of thy line.

III.

Though on thy brow there's traces still of war,
And on thy heart there's many a festering scar,
That time hath healed not, nor can ever heal
While native millions to the stranger kneel.

IV.

Yet these but serve thee as the signal lights,
That show how thou wert plundered of thy rights,
That tell thee, too, that there were always hands
And faithful hearts to guard thy native lands.

V.

Ages of tyranny that would have crushed
The vastest empire have only hushed
Thy native voice, until that voice grew loud,
And strong, and deep, as a charged thundercloud.

VI.

.And as it swept resistlessly along,
It woke the mountain zephyrs with a song
Of Hope and Freedom, till the emerald blaze
Reflected back the "light of long-lost days.'

VII.

Too long thou'st knelt and prayed, but prayed in vain,
To knaves and despots to shake off thy chain!
Thou'lt never kneel or bend again to those
Who've proved thy darkest, deepest, deadliest foes.

VIII.

No, thou hast spoken with a nation's might,
And shook thy chains and dared them to the fight!
They heard and trembled: then with subtle art
They sought to wound thee through thy chieftain's heart.[49]

IX.

'Tis now alike to thee whate'er they do,—
Be just or tyrannous, false friends or true,
They ne'er can wipe away that odious blot,
Through weal or woe it ne'er shall be forgot!

No. 27.

TO IRELAND, WEEP NO MORE.

(Impromptu.)

Written after reading the sentence pronounced on Smith O'Brien.

I.

Weep no more! the hour for sorrow
   Is for ever now gone by;
Draw the sword! your chieftain follow
   Bravely conquer thou or die!—
   Conquer bravely, then, or die!

II.

What care we for graves all gory?—
   What care we for traitors' name;
Conquer and bright wreaths of glory
   Will surround us as a flame—
   Will surround each hallow'd name!

III.

Ask not now the time or season
   When a nation should arise;
But remember the worst treason
   Is to cease to fraternise!
   Be firm, true, and fraternise!

IV.

Men of Leinster, be consistent;
  Men of Munster, firm and bold;
Men of Connaught, be resistant;
  Ulster, look to days of old!
  Ulster, and bright days of old!

V.

Emulate the bright example
  Left you by the nations round!
Snap the chain! on tyrants trample
  Or be slaves for ever bound—
  Crouching slaves for ever bound!

VI.

Weep no more! the hour for sorrow
  Is for ever now gone by;—
Draw the sword! your chieftain follow,
  Bravely conquer, then, or die!
  Conquer bravely then, or die!

No. 28.
SPEAK SOFTLY.

I.

SPEAK softly, lest that radiant form
  Should vanish from my sight,
For she has been, through every storm,
  Life's mildly-guiding light.

II.

And when around me all was dark,
  And tumult filled my breast,
She was the dove of this tossed ark
  That brought me peace and rest!

III

Like eastern mariners, that burn
  Sweet incense to their star,
So does my heart in silence turn
  And worship her afar.

IV.

And yet I never breathe her name
  Nor ask, scarce wish her mine,
But bask within that bright'ning flame
  Which glows from Beauty's shrine!

No. 29.

THE INVADER.

I.

In distant times a stranger knight,
  Whose deeds of blood and crime
Appalled the bravest in the fight,
  Came to bright Mona's Isle.

The bloodhound sent upon the track
    Of the fleet mountain roe,
A wolf-dog fierce in the attack,
    The bold, remorseless foe,
He came; and, like the desert's blast
    Upon the smiling plain,
Where'er his wandering footsteps past
    Nought ever smiled again!

II.

He came with battle-axe and brand,
    And many a targe and spear,
To war 'gainst virtue, fatherland,
    And all the heart holds dear:
To crush the weak and innocent,
    To succour all that's base,
To hurl from Freedom's battlement
    The fine old native race,
That reigned for twice two thousand years,
    In Mona's halls of shell,
And steered the bark through smiles and tears
    So long—it tells how well!

III.

He came: and future times will curse
    His country and his name;
For years the bruised heart will nurse
    The memory of its shame,

Until the iron bonds that bind
    The slave shall snap in twain,
And Erin, rising with one mind
    And heart, shall live again !
Or failing in the dire attack,
    At least will show the way
That liberty can be won back
    Upon some future day !

IV.

He came !—and ere the twilight hour
    Had faded o'er the bay,
He sought the lonely, rocky bower,
    Where Mona's chieftain lay ;
And like the murderous gosshawk's raid
    Upon the stock-dove's nest,
Full furious flashed the glittering blade
    Before the old man's breast :
When a young maiden wildly sprung
    Between the foeman's spear
And that aged form to which she clung,
    And clasped her father dear !

No. 30.

SONG.

From the Dead Man's Chair.

[The Dead Man's Chair is the name of the highest point on Croghan Mountain, anciently called Croghan Kinsellah, situated in the present county of Wicklow. It was the supposed scene of one of the Bardic Sessions, held by the song-writers of the *Wexford Independent.*]

The author addresses the assembled children of song—"Bards! I was requested, on the evening before we assembled, to give a love song by one, beautiful as Moore's ideal, Hinda :—

> "Pure as angel shapes that bless
> Infant dreams, but nothing less
> Rich in all woman's loveliness."

But I cannot attempt it *now*. My heart is sad and my spirits sunk. I have not even thought of a song on any subject; I must, therefore, beg your acceptance of my unpremeditated lay, prompted by the feelings of the moment. Hear my song from the Dead Man's Chair :—

I.

O KATHLIN ! though you made me say
I'd sing a song of love to-day,
And told me, with a rosy smile,
That some young daughter of our isle,
Whose eyes with love's mild lustre beam,
Should be my next inspiring theme :
Alas ! my love, I cannot now—
There's grief upon my heart and brow.

I've touched my harp-strings, one by one,
But all their lively tones are gone:
Plaintive and sad with grief and care
Must be my song from the *Dead Man's Chair*.

II.

And yet, if aught could 'wake this soul
To love and beauty's soft control,
'Tis thee, sweet sunbeam of the heart,
That shines more bright as joys depart,
Like Love's own planet in the west,
That's loveliest when the sun's at rest,
And pours, through broken clouds of even,
The light caught on the verge of heaven!
But sorrow gathers round my breast,
Like mists upon the mountain's crest,
Ah, no! of nothing bright or fair
Must be my song from the *Dead Man's Chair*.

III.

Yet, there is many a charming vale,
The scene of legend, song, and tale,
Where fairies danced, old people say,
And revel kept till break of day;
And though there's many a swelling flood
Which drank the dying patriot's blood,
And many a hill and vale appears
That bristled once with native spears—

Arklow and *Gorey* are in view,[50]
And *Oulart* has its memories too !—
But these are of the things that were,
Still sad my song from the *Dead Man's Chair*.

IV.

Oh ! what avails it now to tell
Of those who conquered or who fell ?—
It would not take one pang away,
Or make the sunk heart light to-day.
After the carnage, blood, and strife,
And all that reckless waste of life,
What better, happier, are we now,
Standing on Croghan's lonely brow ?
Oh ! are not still more galling chains
Our sole inheritance and gains ?
In vain I've sought for something there
To cheer my song from the *Dead Man's Chair*.

V.

What though the streamlets where we stand
Roll over beds of golden sand,
And many an exhaustless mine
Lies hid within its rocky shrine ;
What though each rich and fertile field
Abundant fruits is brought to yield ?
Have we not seen them leave our strand,
While *Famine* wildly stalks the land ?

While millions cried for bread in vain,
'Twas bartered by unholy gain:
Of gloom, regret, and dark despair
Must be my song from the *Dead Man's Chair*.

VI.

And have we not this morning hung
In rapture on the words that sprung,
Deep, powerful, scathing in their force,
As is the burning lava's course,
From one who knows his country well,[51]
The legend of each rock and dell,
Each deed and tale of former times,
Their glory, chivalry, and crimes?
Has he not said that rapine, fraud,
And murder are the things they laud?
Oh! not one flower of hope is there
To twine with my song from the *Dead Man's Chair*.

No. 31.
COME LET US PLEDGE.

[At an imaginary Bardic Session, supposed to be held on the *Royal Hill of Tara*, on the spot called the "Croppies' Grave," the following verses were addressed by the author to the assembled bards, the poetical contributors to the *Independent*.]

I.
COME let us pledge before yon mound,
  The "Croppies' Grave" of ninety-eight,
Let minstrels' harps once more resound
  Above the silent *Stone of Fate*.[53]

II.
Come, *Donald*, pour thy glowing line,
  In thy soft strains of witchery;
What harp, what voice, so fit as thine
  To sing the requiem of the free?

III.
Let *Cormac*, of the "single string,"
  Give us a deep and burning lay;
And o'er us like enchantment fling
  The splendours of an ancient day.

IV.
And *Shemus*, with the sage's art,
  And all the youthful poet's fire,
Come, warm, instruct, delight the heart
  Or rouse it against Saxon ire!

V.

O *Mary*! gifted child of song,
  Awake thy tender, melting strain,
That, raptured, wafts the soul along
  The shining track of hope again!

VI.

Let *Eveleen's* sweet numbers tell
  Of mountain stream and moonlit grove,
Of aged thorn, and fairy dell,
  And the wild haunts of peace and love!

VII.

Now let the *Exile's* master-hand
  Sweep boldly o'er the trembling wire,
And with bright dreams of fatherland
  The coldest hearts with love inspire!

VIII.

Juvernicus, awake thy strains,
  With sword half-sheathed and half-drawn,
Let those old consecrated fanes
  Be first to catch young Freedom's dawn.

IX.

Glenalvon, weave each glowing line
  Above the unforgotten brave;
With one sweet wreath of song entwine
  The heroes of the "Croppies' Grave."

X.

The *Peasant* next, with feelings strong,
 And soul that cannot brook the chain,
Will tune the harp to Freedom's song,
 While Slavery's footprints here remain.

XI.

Raymond of *Forth*, thy pastoral lay
 So sweetly redolent of spring,
Reminds us of a former day,
 And all its glories round us fling.

XII.

Come, let us pledge before yon mound,
 The Croppies' Grave of ninety-eight;
Let minstrel harps once more resound
 Above the silent Stone of Fate!

No. 32
LAMENT

For not knowing the Irish Language, addressed to the Bards assembled in Bardic Session at the grave of the celebrated giant, Diarmuid O'Duibhne, in Barmoney, Co. Wexford.

I.

OH! ask me not to sing to-day,
My heart, my soul is far away
 With other tunes;

My harp's unstrung, my voice is weak,
Let Cormac, Shemus, Donald speak,
Or Mary thoughts of splendour wake
    In glorious rhymes.

II.

But let me pass among the throng,
Nor ask for ballad, tale, or song
    O'er Diarmuid's breast;
If I have touched with trembling hand
The wild harp on my native strand,
The *words* were of the Saxon's land,
    But ill-expressed.

III.

Alas! I do not know the tongue
My father to his proud harp sung
    For king and chief;
That voice is hushed, those strains are o'er,
The bards appear in hall no more,
They sunk amid their country's gore,
    And chains, and grief!

IV.

Those strains that oft in moonlight hour,
Rose soft and sweet from lady's bower,
    And haunted grove,

No longer give unmixed delight
To lady fair and crested knight,
Nor breathe in banquet-hall of light
    The soul of love.

V.

That language in whose depth there dwells
A tenderness that throws its spells
    Around the soul,
Drawing into its magic ring
Each hope that earth left withering,
And making an eternal spring
    Light up the soul;

VI.

Or bursting like the earthquakes' shock
From lonely glen or beetling rock,
    Spreads terror round;
While trampled plume and cloven crest,
And broken lance and bleeding breast,
And many a dying warrior pressed
    The gory ground.

VII.

But, oh! that language scares no more
The tyrant from our native shore
    With battle cry;
And yet, neglected as thou art,
I still could take thee to my heart,
And prize thee as the brightest part
    Of times gone by.

VIII.

Yes, yes, though persecuted long,
Thy spirit lives enthroned in song,
    And yet will blaze
When love and vengeance shall inspire
Some native bard to strike the wire,
And call forth all the latent fire
    Of other days.

IX.

Brothers, I'm done, this lowly strain
May never more be heard again
    By hill or dell;
Farewell! my heart is with the past,
My words are weak—at random cast
My heart is Erin's to the last,
    Farewell! farewell

No. 33.
TO S.

I.

As music on the moonlight sea,
When souls are tuned to melody,
Sends forth each trembling note afar
To you, bright twinkling, evening star;
So does my soul in transport fly
To that lov'd star—this bright black eye.

II.

And as that evening star so bright,
When mildly shining o'er our sight,
Sheds richer lustre then by far
Than any other little star;
So does that bright black eye of thine
All others thus in love outshine.

No 34.

THE VISION.—PART FIRST.

SCENE: *The wild and romantic mountains of Derrynane Abbey—O'Connell alone in deep meditation on the mountains.*—TIME: *A fine evening in autumn.*

I.

A BLUE-EYED maiden meekly knelt
 Before an aged chief,
Her cheeks were pale—for, oh! she felt
 A pang of secret grief.
There, silent, sad, and eloquent,
 The advocate appears,
Like some angelic visitant
 From heaven's golden sphere,
A flowing robe of brightest green
 Comprised her simple dress;
And yet no crowned and sceptred queen
 Showed half such loveliness.

A wreath of shamrocks decked her hair,
  Over a harp she bent,
Then smiling, touched its strings, and now
  Commenced her wild lament:

II.

"My hope, my pride, my guardian-love,
  I've sought thee in thy wild retreat,
Where sublime mountains rise above,
  And smiling vales bloom at thy feet;—
Here, here at least thy soul is free,
  Where all is wild, majestic, grand.
The winds and waves chant liberty
  E'en upon this lonely strand.
'Twas here I first upon thee smiled,
  And held aloft my broken chain;
Then thou didst vow, in accents wild,
  My long-lost freedom to regain!
There thou didst call me thy own love,
  Thy beautiful confiding bride,
And 'twas in vain my rivals strove,
  Since then to win thee from my side.
In vain they sought thee to forsake
  The weeping slave that o'er thee bent,
Well thou didst know my heart would break
  To find thee, too, a recreant.
There thou hast stood through good and ill,
  A light, an oracle, a guide,
Guarding, instructing, cheering still,
  But never from my love divide.

I gave thee all—my confidence,
  My strength, my love, though poor, was sweet;
My hopes, my heart, burning intense,
  All, all were cast beneath thy feet.
Oh! say then am I now less thine,
  Than when thou'st took me to thy heart,
And vowed that both through storm and shine,
  Let come what would we'd never part!
Is beauty faded from my cheek?
  Is this poor heart grown changed and cold?
My love, instructor, guardian, speak!—
  Am I not as I was of old?
Oh! no; my massive chains were rent,
  My bonds were broken too by thee;
But sure 'twas never thy intent
  To give me but half-liberty!" [53]

No. 35.

THE VISION.—PART SECOND.

O'Connell's reply to the Genius of Erin.

I.

BEAUTIFUL being, let me gaze
  Entranced upon thy heavenly brow,
For never did its magic blaze
  Shine half so brilliantly as now.

No, not in boyhood's highest dream
   Of bliss when first I felt thy power,
Did'st thou so pure, so lovely seem,
   As thou dost in this very hour:
Sweet as the summer breeze that plays
   O'er fragrant shrubs of Thomond's highlands;
Pure as the evening beam that strays
   Among Killarney's fairy islands;
Soft as the fabled towers that shine
   Beneath the waves of Lough Neagh's waters,
Rich as the Liffey's golden mine
   Art thou the pride of western daughters.
Oh! gentle as the Slaney's tide
   Ere tempests lash it into billows;
Oh! lovely as the streams that glide
   By moonlight through Avoca's willows;
Majestic as Slieve Donard's peak,
   That stays the flashing lightning's pinion;
O Erin! sure my heart would break
   To see thee bow to foreign minion!
Forsake thee!—no, thou art my pride!
   And while one galling chain remains,
My place is ever by thy side,
   To tear away thy servile chains.
Thou art too beautiful, too brave,
   Too full of life and energy,
To bear the bond of serf or slave
   When thou couldst with one bound be free!

But guided by the fearful past,
   Which sheds a dim, but warning light,
We will not hazard by a cast
   Thy destiny till *all unite.*
'Twas this that caused me to invite
   Thy sons of every class and creed
To join me in the moral fight,
   Or show me how thou might'st be freed.
They came not, but be their's the fault,
   Be their's the folly and disgrace;
I warned, invited, but did nought
   To cause me now to shun thy face,
And though some cold hearts still remain
   Still hostile to thy just demand,
God! can the millions speak in vain
   Who love thee and their fatherland?
Have they not seen, have we not felt
   Our country's ruin and decay,
Since first our native princes knelt,
   And bound their necks to Norman sway?
Yes; like the deadly Upas-tree,
   That sheds its poisonous vapours round,
They turned to wild sterility
   This Eden of enchanting ground!

No 36.

I LOVE THE SONGS OF IRELAND.

I.

I LOVE the songs of Ireland,
   For deep in each one dwells
The memory of a thousand years,
   A tenderness that tells
Of deep, enduring, changeless love;
   Of inspiration high,
Which throw a brilliancy across
   Our dark and troubled sky.

II.

I love those strains our princes heard
   In rapture and delight,
When minstrels pour'd the song of love
   In banquet-hall of light;
Where many a pluméd warrior sighed
   Beneath his coat of steel,
And beamy eyes looked down in vain,
   Love's softness to conceal.

III

I love the dear old Irish songs
   Which lead us back again,
Through the wrapt mazes of the mind,
   To some enchanted glen;

Where fairies once more dance beneath
  Their own lov'd favourite tree,[54]
And pour upon the moonlight air
  Their witching minstrelsy.

IV.

I love them, for, like beacon lights
  Above the stormy waves,
They shone throughout our island's wreck
  O'er martyred patriots' graves;
Nor demon hate, nor dastard fear,
  Nor cold neglect, nor time,
Nor treachery could quench those lights
  Which burn still, clear—sublime.

Sentimental Songs.

No. 1.

SONG.

I CANNOT SING OF LOVE TO-NIGHT.

I.

I CANNOT sing of love to-night,
   My soul is tuned to notes of sadness;
Not even thy blue eyes of light
   Can bring to me one moment's gladness.
The wine-cup shines for me in vain,
   And music magic sweetness stealing
O'er this lone heart but brings it pain
   And stirs anew the fount of feeling,
Which, gushing o'er the burning waste
   Of blighted hopes and lost affections,
Ah, no; I never more can taste
   The Eden of youth's recollections.

II.

As some poor mariner that sees,
  When daylight in the west's declining,
A phantom isle on halcyon seas
  In all its fairy splendour shining ;
But when he nears its golden peaks,
  A change comes o'er its trembling motion,
The lovely, baseless vision breaks
  And melts into the depths of ocean !
So fade away my dreams of bliss
  That threw their passing splendours o'er me,
That shone awhile before my sight,
  Then quickly vanished from before me !

No. 2.
O KATHLEEN ! GUARD, OH ! GUARD THY HEART.

I.

O KATHLEEN ! guard, oh ! guard thy heart
  From life's deep, poisonous sting ;
Dare to be guileless as thou art
  Now in thy opening spring.

II.

And when thy beauty shall have passed
  Forever from thy brow ;—
Oh ! may thy young heart's bloom still last
  As tenderly as now.

III.

See how the summer steals away
　　The rose's brightest bloom,
But cannot, even in decay
　　Destroy its rich perfume.

IV.

So may thy soul through life retain
　　Its sweets when years have passed,
Without a shade or cloud to stain
　　Its odour to the last.

No. 3.

OH! TURN AWAY THOSE EYES OF LIGHT.

I.

OH! turn away those eyes of light,
　　Since they can never beam for me:
Thy smile though sweet, thy brow though
　　　bright;
Again can never bless my sight,
　　Young love, for I must part from thee.

II.

Long, long I've tried to stand unmoved,
  But, ah, I found it could not be!
Each moment but too truly proved
How fond, how fervently I loved,
  Nay, more then loved, I worshipped thee!

III.

Yes, I have sat the livelong hour
  Indulging dreams of ecstasy;
And if dark thoughts would sometimes lower,
With one bright smile thou had'st the power
  To win them back again to thee.

IV.

Ah, then, I knew not that the shrine
  At which I prayed and bent the knee,
The things I lov'd and dreamed divine,
My country, freedom, all that twine
  Around me were despised by thee.

V.

But now I feel that we must part,
  Whate'er may be my destiny!
Yet, never shall that light depart
From out this blighted, bleeding heart,
  Which memory links with love and thee!

VI.

Farewell ! though heaven were in thy smile
   And bliss in thy soft melody,
I would not be a wretch so vile
   As to forsake my emerald isle
     Even to gain the love of thee !

No. 4.
CHILD OF CLAY.

I.

Child of clay, dost thou remember
   That the summer soon flies past,
And that bleak and dark December
   Unawares steals on at last ?
Thus it is that life's young morning
   Is o'ershadowed e'er with care,
And the bloom thy cheek adorning
   Will be transitory there.

II.

Now the world is fresh before thee,
   And each day adds something new,
Lovers lived but to adore thee !
   Friends seem ever kind and true !
But the heart soon finds that sorrow
   Mingles with its happiness,
And when each succeeding morrow
   Comes it finds a joy the less.

III.

Do not believe the earth can ever
   Satisfy the human heart,
Fondest, dearest ties must sever,
   Truest friends must one day part;
Seek then in yon heaven above us
   Joys which suffer no decay,
Where they bloom with those who love us
   In realms of never-ending day!

No. 5.

TO MARY, AFTER A LONG ABSENCE.

I

MARY I feel my spirit steal
   Over the waste of years and hours,
Which seem to throw an envious veil
   O'er Memory's brightest, fairest flowers.

II.

Mary, they cannot;—years may roll,
   Till youth and loveliness be over,
But still within this changeless soul
   Shall glow the flame of a young lover.

III.

Mary, we lov'd in life's young spring,
   When all was mirth, and joy, and gladness,
When vivid fancy lov'd to fling
   Her fairy beams unmixed with sadness.

IV.

Mary, since then this heart is changed,
  To all it ever lov'd or hated;
From thee alone 'tis not estranged,
  From thee 'twill ne'er be separated,

No. 6.

MY OWN DEAR GIRL.

I.

My own dear girl, though bright thy smile
  As light on roses;
Though pure thy heart and free from guile
  Where love reposes;
And though thy mild, madonna eye
  Is full of feeling,
Not these, *not* these could wake one sigh
  When to thee kneeling.

II.

Thy souls rich sunshine sweetly plays
  Around thee ever,
Like gems in some transparent vase
  Whose brightness never
Is dimmed, or changed, or turned apart
  Though darkness lower:
But this, not this could touch the heart
  With love's soft power.

III.

'Tis not thy sylph-like form that flings
    Its magic round me,
'Tis not thy bright imaginings
    That ever bound me!
And though thy voice is soft and full
    Of deep emotion,
These could not win, though beautiful,
    My heart's devotion.

IV.

I've heard thee sigh, when thou hast read
    From native pages,
How much poor Ireland fought and bled
    Through long, long ages;
I've seen thee shed the big bright tear
    O'er cross and cairn,
These, *these* have made thee ever dear,
    Young maid of Erin!

No. 7.
I SAW THY KINDLING BEAUTIES SHINE.

I.

I SAW thy kindling beauties shine
  In splendid corruscations o'er thee,
And, dazzled by so fair a shrine,
  I paused not then, but bowed before thee.

II.

I knew not then, I know not now,
  What 'twas that caused this heart's devotion;
I only know and feel that thou
  Has been the cause of this emotion.

III.

I felt thy beauty, still I dreamed
  This heart could stand unmoved as ever,
But so much radiance round me gleamed,
  That heart and soul were gone forever!

IV.

I knew not, cared not, for I felt
  The rosy tint of love around me,
And, reckless of the future, knelt
  A captive to the spell that bound me.

No. 8.

THE DAYS OF YOUTH.

I.

The days, the happy days of youth,
  When life was in its spring,
And every face beamed love and truth,
  And joy was on the wing :
Oh ! then the flowers were fresh and fair,
  The fields and meadows gay,
The heart was light and free from care
  The live-long summer's day.

II.

But soon, too soon, a chilling change
   Comes o'er the glowing heart:
Friends, joys seem heartless, cold, and strange
   As boyhood days depart;
The world is not that place of bliss
   And love it used to be:
We scarce can recognise in this
   Our world of infancy.

III.

Ah, no; the charm soon fades away
   Like sunshine in the west,
And with it these fond hopes decay
   And die within the breast.
But even now a voice or flower,
   Or music's simple strain,
That we have lov'd in childhood's hour,
   Can make all bright again!

No. 9.

"GO NOT AWAY"

"'Tis sad to change, when what is, *is* so delightful."

I.

Go not away! we must not part,
Let this poor spoiled romantic heart

Still dream the world is full of bliss,
Of beauty, love, and happiness,
As it does when I near thee stray,
Then do not—*do* not go away.

II.

Like some poor bird with weary wing,
That flies, about in quest of spring,
But, finding neither flower nor leaf,
It pines away in secret grief:
So would I mourn both night and day,
Dear friend, if thou wouldst go away.

III.

Ah, yes! and this neglected lute
Would be for ever sad and mute;
How could I give those songs again
We've sung together in the glen?—
And who would praise my little lay
When thou wouldst be far, far away!

IV.

When thou art near I do not mind
The coldness of a world unkind,
Nor miss the rich and glorious beam
Of summer from the flower or stream,
Nor see I the bright rose decay,—
Then go not, ah, go not away!

No. 10.

THOUGH FEELING.

I.

Though feeling is a painful thing
   That wakes the soul to sadness,
And o'er life's path does often fling
A bloom that leaves us withering
   Without one gleam of gladness.

II.

Yet, give me one that takes a part
   Alike in joy and sorrow,
Who feels the bright poetic start
Or every feeling of the heart
   That gilds or shades each morrow.

III.

Yes, give me one whose hopes are gone,
   Whose young affection's blighted,
Who finds the hallow'd light that shone
Around him as he journeyed on
   Has left him quite benighted,

IV.

For memory then will often cling
   To former ties that bound us,
And strike a sympathetic string,
Whose tones with soft awakening
   Then throw a halo round us.

V.

Though cold philosophy may dream
  It frivolous and idle,
Oh ! give me still the poet's dream,
The saunter by the willow stream
  And thoughts too strong to bridle.

VI.

Thus let me glide unheeded on
  Unseen among the willows
A stranger to those gems that shone
Like lights on Indian streams that one
  By one went down the billows !

No. 11.

OH, WOULD I WERE A CHILD AGAIN.

I.

OH ! would I were a child again,
  Still playing on the spangled green,
Or musing by that rocky glen [55]
  On what I'm now or might have been.

II.

On what I'm now !—oh, did I e'er
  In thought or feeling dream to be
So soon oppressed with anxious care,
  With joy and grief alternately.

III.

What was I then?—a careless child,
    A bark upon a sunny sea,
That o'er young life's stream sweetly smiled
    Until the bark sailed far away.

IV.

But soon, too soon, that bark was tossed
    By wild waves o'er the trackless main,
And when each hope and light was lost,
    The bark could not return again.

V.

'Twas thus upon life's checquered stream
    Each hope and feeling soon was given;
But light at first, as heaven's beam,
    Then dark as clouds by thunders riven!

VI.

What am I now? I scarce can tell,
    A wild weed waving in the blast,
A blighted branch, a ceaseless knell,
    That speaks of all that's bright and past.

No. 12.
WHEN THE FIRST SMILING BEAMS OF DAY.

I.

WHEN the first smiling beams of day
    Break over tree and flower,
Oh! then how pleasant 'tis to stray
    In that enchanting hour;

Though I have lov'd the morning's light,
  Sparkling with pearly dew,
It never more can bring delight,
  If not enjoyed with you.

II.

And when mild evening melts along
  The purple heather hills,
Oh! then the blackbird's mellow song
  A happiness instils;
And yet, it cannot touch this heart
  Nor eve's own heavenly hue
To me no bliss can e'er impart
  If not enjoyed by you.

III.

When loves own planet shone above
  Like some bright isle of bliss,
Ah, once 'twas sweet to me to rove
  In such an hour as this;
But now the most bewitching ray
  That beams through skies of blue
Can never make this spirit gay
  If not enjoyed with you.

IV.

There is another hour which flings
  Sweet happiness around,
When each enchanted moment brings
  Fresh gifts from fairy ground;

'Tis when the silent moon shines bright
  And cares are light and few,
And yet it cannot bring delight
  If not enjoyed with you.

No. 13.

OH! WILT THOU GIVE ME BACK MY HEART?

I.

OH! wilt thou give me back my heart,
  Or keep, oh! keep it safe for me?
For, young and lovely as thou art,
  I could not, could not leave it thee,
To be the idol of an hour,
  And then to fling it idly by,
Like some neglected little flower
  That's plucked and left to fade and die.

II.

Yes, give, oh! give me back my heart
  Though Love's wild passion flower shall fade,
'Twere better far that we should part
  If thou canst trifle still, dear maid!
For though thy smile's bewitching ray
  Now beams uncloudedly on me,
All may be changed and dark next day,
  And then—'twere death to leave it thee!

No. 14.

TO AGNES.

I.

Oh, that I had never met thee!
    Never gazed upon thy brow;
Then at least I'd ne'er regret thee,
    And this heart were tranquil now!
But too oft I've sat before thee,
    And enjoyed thy gentle smile,
Which in brightness oft broke o'er me,
    Like sweet moonlight o'er our isle!
Yes, too long, too well I loved thee,
    As this throbbing heart can tell,
And though nought I prize above thee,
    Must I, can I say farewell!

II.

Is this dream of splendour broken
    Which entranced my heart and mind?
Gone, without the slightest token,
    Save the pain it leaves behind.
Am I never more to see thee,
    But like those who ne'er had met?
Yet in dreams I will be near thee,
    Busy memory can't forget!

Were the whole world's gaudy treasure
Placed this moment at my will,
I would spurn it for the pleasure
To be with thee—near *thee* still!

No. 15.
TO M.

I.

A BIRD that beats its little wings
   Against its cage, and tries to flee
To its own native woodland springs
Where still its wild companion sings,
   Is like what I am without thee!

II.

An exile, whose deep, anxious gaze
   Is turned across the broad, blue sea,
To his loved home of childhood's days,
Where memory oft in day-dreams strays,
   Is like what I am without thee!

III.

A long-neglected garden, where
   Not one lone tree or flower may be
Now seen, although things rich and rare,
And beautiful once flourished there,
   Is like what I am without thee!

IV.

A soul whose last sweet hope is gone,
  A faded flower, a blighted tree,
A broken heart that still beats on,
When things that long around it shone
Have all departed one by one,
  Are like what I am without thee

No. 16.
STANZAS.

I.

'Twas not thy starry eye, though bright
And shining like those orbs of light
So gloriously in heaven at night,
    That taught me first to love thee!

II.

'Twas not thy smile's bewitching ray,
Bright as the beams of opening day
When dancing o'er the waves in play,
    That taught me first to love thee!

II.

'Twas not thy lip, like the young rose,
When the first hour it opening blows,
And all its fresh young charms disclose,
    That taught me first to love thee!

IV.

'Twas not thy brow nor forehead fair,
Nor yet thy simply-braided hair,
That hangs in dark-brown tresses there,
    That taught me first to love thee!

V.

'Twas not thy teeth of polished sheen,
Flashing like ocean spars, between
The sweetest lips that e'er were seen,
    That taught me first to love thee!

VI.

'Twas not thy bosom's rising swell,
Where pure and gentle feelings dwell,
That round me threw their fairy spell
    And taught me how to love thee!

VII.

'Twas not thy lips, thy teeth, thine eye,
Thy hair, thy bosom, or thy sigh,
It was, in truth, I know not why,
    I only know I love thee!

No. 17.

STANZAS TO * * * *

I.

I'll think of thee when morning's beam
    Sheds its first tint on summer sky;
I'll think of thee in every dream
    That brings a smile or wakes a sigh.

II.

I'll think of thee when evening's sun
    Is sinking in the ocean fast,
I'll think of thee when murmurs run
    Along its wild and stormy blast,

III.

I'll think of thee in every prayer
    Of kindred and of claim;
And heaven will soothe the falling tear,
    When mingled with thy name.

IV.

I'll think of thee when life's last gleam
    Has vanished from my breast,
When every fading thought and scene
    Sinks to eternal rest!

No. 18.

SONG.

OH, THINK OF ME!

I.

Oh, think of me in that sweet time,
When vesper breathes its parting chime,
And sunlight throws its last farewell
Upon our lonely, quiet dell;
Where thoughts fly back like the fond dove
To its dear home of peace and love;
When whispering feelings tell to thee
Fond dream of love—then think of me!

II.

Oh, think of me in that lone hour,
When moonlight sheds its magic power,
Like lovers' glances half-way hid
Beneath the downcast, shaded lid;
And when around thee all is gay,
Oh, think of someone far away,
And softly breathe that none may hear,
"Oh, how I wish that *he* were here!"

No. 19.

SONG.

THERE'S NONE LIKE THEE.

I.

Oh! there are visions pure and bright
   Which sometimes throw a mystic spell
Around our busy thoughts at night,
   More beautiful than words can tell;
And there are day-dreams that oft steal
   Around the heart enchantingly,
But 'mid that galaxy, I feel,
   However bright, there's none like thee!

II.

I've seen some lovely forms that made
   A circling radiance o'er the soul,
Soft as a moonlight serenade,
   Whose sweetness every moment stole
Into the heart, in that lone hour,
   When love, and light, and minstrelsy
Unite with all their fairy power,
   But still I find there's none like thee!

III.

I've met some, too, whose glancing eyes
   Shone like the glittering diamond's blaze,
Whose bright, clear depths all but defies
   The soul that turns to meet their gaze;

And some, whose soft tones sent a thrill
Of sweet, bewildering ecstasy,
Into the heart which lives there still—
But yet, there's none, there's none like thee!

No. 20.

STANZAS TO ELLEN.

I MET THEE IN LIFE'S EARLY PRIME.

I.

I MET thee in life's early prime, ere a shade
Of this cold world darkened thy way:
Young, lovely, and artless, bright smiles round thee played,
Like sunshine o'er flowers in May.
All beaming with gladness, and sparkling with youth,
Oh! 'tis joy but to be where thou art,
And hear those lov'd accents of candour and truth
Come guilelessly forth from the heart!

II.

With thee were my thoughts from the earliest dawn;
And in dreams thy bright form I see;
Not a shape of deep beauty my fancy has drawn
But are all glowing portraits of thee!

Enchantress! 'tis thou all my soul dost inspire
With love-light of music and song;
To love and to thee I've awakened my lyre,
For to thee heart and lyre belong!

No. 21.

SONG.

COME WANDER BY THE VALLEY'S WELL.

I.

Come wander by the valley's well,
    Where fairies dance so lightly;
Come through the lonely hazel dell,
    Where the summer moon shines brightly;
We'll stray beside the haunted stream,
    And under the banshee-thorn,
Until the starlight's dewy beam
    Fades in the beam of morn!

II.

There's not a beauteous bird that flies
    Among earth's fairest flowers;
There's not a spirit 'neath the skies
    That plays in twilight bowers;

SENTIMENTAL SONGS.

Or roams delightedly above
  The clouds, the air, or water,
Shall feel more ecstasy, my love,
  Than I with earth's fair daughter!

III.

We'll count each star in heaven to-night
  That o'er us now is beaming,
We'll watch each glorious spirit's flight
  With streaks of brightness gleaming:
And as we turn to earth we'll dream
  Our pathway thus all glowing,
With love we'll shed as sweet a beam
  As those that heaven's bestowing!

No. 22.

SONG.

NEVER! OH, NEVER AGAIN CAN THIS HEART.

I.

NEVER! oh, never again can this heart
  Feel the pulse of the rapture thy presence once gave
No more may I feel that pure ecstatic start
  Which in tumult broke o'er me like wave over wave!

II.

The life of wild rapture has died in my breast,
  Like the fragrance of flowers that passes away:
Let them be e'er so bright, oh! the more they are pressed,
  The sooner they wither and suffer decay.

III.

The bloom of the heart never withers, 'tis said,
  While the fields of enjoyment are still in our view;
But 'tis false—for I feel that all mine is now fled,
  Though basking in sunlight of smiles still from you.

IV.

The rose when it withers may hang on its tree,
  And, though warmed with sunshine, and watered with dew,
And though all around it enchanting may be,
  These never again can its fragrance renew.

V.

The mirror, once broken and severed, can ne'er
  Reflect back a feature though ever so bright,
But a thousand small, indistinct figures are there,
  Mere fragments of beauty that ne'er can unite!

VI.

Thus severed, and broken, and withered, this heart
  Cannot feel those enchantments thy presence once
    gave;
No more can I feel that pure ecstatic start
  Which in rapture broke o'er me like wave over
    wave!

No. 23.

LINES TO * * * *

AH! do not doubt the poet's vow,
  Though breathed in passion's deep excess;
He cannot love thee more than now,
  And feels he ne'er can love thee less.
His love is like the sweet night flower,
  That cannot bear the blaze of day,
But in eve's soft and silent hour
  It sighs its fragrant soul away;
Or like the desert's secret spring
  That tends one lone and lovely tree,
When all around lie withering
  And sad as I am without thee!
Oh! 'tis not in the lighted hall,
  Where song and music float around,
And love's own accents seem to fall;
  But, ah! not there true love is found;

As soon might you expect to see
    The flowers that gave their scent away,
Bloom fresh, and fair, and fragrantly
    On the neglected wreath next day,
As find amid the heartless throng
    A soul of flame and constancy,
Deep, pure, refined, exalted, strong,
    To feel as I have felt for thee.
No, no, 'tis in the lonely hour,
    When evening sheds her golden beams
That love's low whisperings have power
    To touch the heart like fairy dreams,
Whose radiance sparkles over all
    Life's varied actions to the last,
And turns to light as they recall
    Thoughts of the bright and glowing past.
I grant the world may sometimes break
    Love's image from a heart most true,
But when the storm is past, the lake
    Reflects the flowers that o'er it grew,
Bright, calm, and tranquil—the same
    As if no tempest ever came;
And so does love return at length,
    With all its wonted power and strength!

No 24.

SONNET

To Mary.

I LOVE thy name, for 'twas my mother's name,
   The first that tingled in my infant ears,
   The first dear sound, too, that in after years,
Absorbed my very being like a flame,
And lit my soul with love's own radiant dream,
Too bright, too beautiful for earth to claim !
   Like the sweet morning star with gentle ray,
   The name of Mary rose upon my way,
Adorning earth, yet shining far above,
   Pure, mild, and bright to manhood's perfect day;
But fiercer then it took the name of love,
   And poured its light in one effulgent blaze—
   A meteor spark that flashed with all its rays—
Oh, that such light as this fades and decays!

No. 25.

TO * * * *

I.

I FONDLY, oh! I deeply thought,
   Thy heart's pure love was mine,
Nor dreamt that feelings could be bought
   So exquisite as thine.

II.

Yes, I once knew thee all my own,
    And never could believe
So kind, so soft, so sweet a tone
    Could me, at least, deceive.

III.

I saw the kindling of thy cheek,
    I heard thy suppressed sigh,
That told a tale thou couldst not speak
    When other forms were by.

IV.

I've marked thy look of tenderness
    That oft in secret stole
Timid and mild, but not the less
    Enchanting to the soul.

V.

Oh, yes, I've felt thy soothing power
    Sink deep into my heart,
Like sunshine streaming on a flower,
    Of which it forms a part!

VI.

And when I pressed thy hand in mine,
    It trembled to the touch;
A thousand little acts of thine
    Told how I was loved much.

VII.

But now I seek in vain for one
    Kind glance like those of old,
Love, friendship from thy bosom's gone,
    All there is changed and cold.

VIII.

You knew I lov'd, but none could tell
    Its depth, its constancy:
But you dissolved the fairy spell,
    And I, once more, am free.

IX.

For worlds I would not again
    Feel that short dream of bliss,
To wake to life and feel the pain
    Of a cold world like this.

X.

Farewell! I can forgive thee all,
    Though every joy is set;
Oh! would I could the past recall,
    Or might at least forget!

No. 26.
FAREWELL.

I.

FAREWELL! farewell, my lovely maid,
A long, a last farewell!
How oft I've struggled to have said,
But not till now could ever breathe
  So sad a parting knell.

II.

Farewell! it flashes o'er my soul
  Like lightnings through yon sky;
And I have said it, and it stole
Like echo's airy notes that roll
  From some lone spirit's cry.

III.

No traces now of grief express
  The soul of feeling fled;
But all is calm and passionless
As marble forms that coldly press
  Above the lordly dead,

IV.

But, ah! one pang still lingers yet,
  Although I've said farewell;
And though my brightest hopes are set,
I feel we never can forget
  When once we lov'd too well.

V.

And what though other years may see
  A form as bright as thine;
It will but tell me still of thee,
And all that was enchantingly,
  But never could be mine.

VI.

When absence tore me from thy side,
  I thought my heart would break;
Since then we've met, but pique or pride
Has served but farther to divide
  Those thoughts you cannot take.

VII.

How oft at evening's fairy hour,
  When mem'ry claims a sigh,
I'll gather every beauteous flower
That ever bloomed in fragrant bower,
  And tend them till they die.

VIII.

And when their fragrance wastes away,
  I'll prize them more than ever;
They'll be too like hope's withering stay,
And hearts that lov'd but yesterday,
  To-morrow waits to sever!

IX.

Although I may no more possess
  A moment's thought of thine,
I cannot, dare not, love thee less,
But cling to all that artlessness
  Which fancy painted mine.

X.

Still let me love, whatever be,
  My errors or my lot,
'Tis passion pure and fervently
That memory links along with thee,
  Remembered or forgot!

No. 27.
MAY.

I

It is the time of flowers,
  When all is bright and gay,
Soft, fragrant, shining hours,
  Oh! 'tis the beautiful sweet May.

II.

Sweet month, around thee ever
  My fondest feelings twine,
Tendrils that nought can sever
  From their lov'd fragrant shrine.

III.

It is a time the metest
  For hearts who love full well,
The brightest, purest, sweetest,
  Those tender thoughts to tell.

IV.

Oh, yes; fond recollections
  Of love without decay;
And dreamy, dim reflections
  Haunt the wrapt soul all day.

V.

When earth and heaven are glowing
  With radiance from above,
What heart is not bestowing
  Its incense of pure love?

VI.

And rainbow-like extending
  An arch of love and light,
Soft, spiritualised, and ending
  In heaven, where all unite!

No. 28.

SONG.

COME, WEND OUR WAY.

I.

Come, wend our way to yonder vale
  Where moonlight's calmly sleeping,
Where fragrance fills the gentle gale,
  And woodbine flowers are weeping;
    The dewdrops bright,
    In heaven's light,
And all is calm and lonely;—
    Come, and thou'lt see
    How sweet 'twill be
To live and love there only!

II.

Thy throne shall be the mossy seat,
  Thy crown the sweet moon glancing
Through flowery boughs, whilst underneath
  The young leaves all are dancing!
    Oh, 'tis an hour,
    When love has power,
In places bright and lonely;—
    Then come and see
    How sweet 'twill be
To live and love there only!

In places bright and lonely;
    Then come and see
    How sweet 'twill be
To live and love there only!

III.

And though there may be scenes more fair,
  And countries as enchanting;
Oh, what would all earth's gifts be there
  If Irish love were wanting!
    The brightest skies,
    Without thine eyes,
Would seem dark, sad, and lonely:
    Come, then, and we
    Shall happy be,
With life and love there only!

No. 29.

THE SONGS OF CHILDHOOD.

I.

DEAR are the songs or childhood,
  For they bring back again
The harebell of the wildwood,
  The cowslip of the glen;

Their shapes, their scents are blending
    With those soft simple airs,
'Tis childhood's heaven descending
    To calm life's feverish cares.

II.

Their melody sheds o'er me
    A tranquil, sweet regret;
Old times then shine before me,
    And friends I can't forget,
From heaven come to greet me
    Whene'er I hear those airs;
Then come, old friends, all meet me
    To calm life's feverish cares.

III.

The song bird once more wildly
    Sings from his haunted brake
While evening's soft light mildly
    Is trembling o'er the lake;
And memory then is dreaming
    Of long-forgotten things,
Oh! 'tis childhood's songs are beaming
    O'er our imaginings!

No. 30.

TO * * * * *

"My life's gladness is gone; I have no more love to give, farewell!—forget me!"—FREDERIKA BREMAR.

I.

For me there's no returning
   Of happy days and festive hours,
One deep thought, ever burning,
     Has snapped the heart's long-cherished flowers;
The rainbow hope I cherished,
   Devotedly for years and years,
Within my bosom perished,
     And left me nought but saddening tears!

II.

No more may life's young gladness
   Light up again this pallid brow,
My soul is turned to sadness,
   And all that's bright forsakes me now.
Within this world now lonely
   My pilgrimage henceforth must be,
Since all life's joy's were only
     One long, bright, blissful dream of thee!

No 31.

TO * * * *

"It was enough for me to be
So near to hear, and, oh! to see
The being whom I loved the most."—

MAZEPPA.

I.

THE moments that I passed with thee
However brief and few they be,
And winged with fears, are doubly dear,
With none save one, to see or hear
The rapture one such moment brings,
Surpassing the imaginings
Of all I ever felt or knew
Of joy until I met with you.

II.

The voice of song I love so well,
And music, too, that throws a spell
Around the soul, soft and sublime;
The flowers I lov'd in childhood's time,
And the sweet intercourse of those
Who long have shared my joys and woes,
Could not such transport e'er impart,
As but to see thee gives this heart!

No 32.

TO JANE.

WOMAN'S EYE.

> " As the stream late concealed
>   In the fringe of its willows,
> When it rushes revealed
>   In the light of its billows ;
> As the bolt burst on high
>   From the black clouds that bound it
> Flashed the soul of that eye
>   Through the long lashes round it !"—
>
> THE BRIDE OF ABYDOS.

I.

THERE is a language in the eye, a spell,
   A secret, silent eloquence that speaks,
Not to the vulgar crowd, but, oh, how well !
   How truly ! to the heart that once awakes
To love and sympathy. Its bright depths tell
Of dream-like thoughts and things unutterable !
For sweeter than the sound that music makes,
   On autumn eves beneath the brilliant moon,
When the poor exile his last farewell takes
   Of home, and all he loves and leaves so soon,
   And the bewildered soul's eclipsed in sorrow's noon !

II.

As stars are called the Poetry of the skies,
　　With glimpses of their glory shining through,
So do the lov'd stars of the soul—thine eyes—
　　Reflect each glowing feeling bright and true;
Yes; in their clear and beamy depths there lies
Each thing the soul could fancy, hope, or prize—
　　Truth, love, and feeling, with emotions new,
And beautiful as evening beams that steal
　　Through variegated clouds away from view,
But even still some varied charms reveal,
　　Transient, as if they sought, but could not all conceal.

III.

Oh, how much do those shining depths express
　　What never could be written, sung, or spoken!
There stands the soul revealed in loveliness,
　　The spirit of the spell she has awoken!
How many thoughts and shapes of beauty press
On the wrapt mind, "like angel forms that bless
　　Infant dreams," until th' enchantment's broken;
But only broken to again combine
　　Some spiritualised idea—some sweet token—
Some *souvenir* of the heart wrenched from the mine
Of the affections all sparkling, rich, and thine!

No. 33.

SONG.

ONE LAST LOOK LET ME FONDLY TAKE.

" Memory will not let go her hold at a bidding; and the heart has a memory of its own."—THE NOWLANS.

I.

One last look let me fondly take,
   Speak but one word as thou hast spoken,
One last embrace, before it break
   My heart—would 'twere already broken!
One sigh still let me breathe to thee
   Before our hearts for aye shall sever:
'Twill be a lonely light to me,
   Of joy that's passed away for ever!

II.

How I have lov'd thee none may know,
   But still within this bosom ever,
Like fires that in the mountain glow,
   Shall burn, unquenched, that flame for ever:
Too long I've worshipped at one shrine,
   Too oft this heart's deep, pure emotion
Of changeless love was breathed to thine,
   To place on others its devotion.

III.

Oh, no! the worshipper that brings
   Fresh offerings still through every danger,
And to one shrine untiring clings,
   Can never bow before the stranger,
Howe'er so beautiful or fair,
   And rich, beyond all earthly dower:
The heart, the heart is too sincere
   To waver for a single hour!

IV.

Though fate has severed far and wide
   Our hearts I once thought nought could sever,
And even against hope relied,
   That love like ours would last for ever!
'Twas useless all, for now I feel
   Such dreams can never more come o'er me;
But memory still will brightly steal
   Around this heart that must adore thee!

No. 34.

FITZSTEPHEN'S SONG.

I.

The morning dawn is breaking,
While my lonely watch I'm keeping,
And the day-star is retreating

Before heaven's bright'ning brow,
Like those early dreams which bound me,
While their splendours shone around me,
Until at last they found me,
    All sad and lonely now !

II.

One by one each hope I cherished,
Each endearing thought I nourished
In my bosom's core hath perished,
    But their memory still is bright.
Like yon distant star, still glowing,
With celestial light whilst going
From the world, is now bestowing
    On earth a long "good-night!"

No. 35.
STANZAS TO MIRZA.
WHEN LAST I MET THEE.

"Earth holds no other like to thee,
And if it did, in vain for me,
*   *   *   *   *   *   *
'Tis all too late—thou wert, thou art,
The cherished madness of this heart."—
                              THE GIAOUR.

I.

WHEN last I met thee, Mirza, on thy face
  A glow of youthful beauty brightly shone,
And innocent delight threw its soft grace
  Over each blushing feature, one by one,

Like stars on summer evenings, I could trace
  Those gushing gleams of tenderness upon
Thy lips, and eyes, and cheeks, and forehead fair,
Making it earthly joy to gaze one moment there!

II.

When gazing there what was the world to me,
  With all its tinsel and unreal joys?—
Its pride, its pomp, its riches! why, to be—
  Blessed with one smile of thine, which never cloys,
Was wealth, power, fame worth immortality.
  But, oh! how oft one day, one hour destroys
The brightest hopes that ever virtue wove
Round faithful hearts in bonds of perfect love.

III.

We met by chance at first, as travellers cast
  Upon the world's broad highway without aim,
Or plan, or purpose, yet a spirit passed
  Into each soul that lighted up a flame,
Which will through life unchangeably still last
  Unseen, perhaps, but ne'er the less the same,
As when it first absorbed each thought and sense,
Pure, brilliant, burning, constant, and intense.

IV.

There is no heart so desolate and lone
  That has not some sweet vision shining there,
Some charmed thought, some idol of its own,
  A standard by which all things bright, and fair,

And beautiful, are judged, and take their tone,
   Like evening clouds floating in upper air,
Which drink the glories of the setting sun,
And stamps his image there when its bright course is run.

V.

Mirza, all this thou wert to me, and more;
   And though our paths through life are severed wide,
And we can never reach that sunny shore
   Which fancy pictured smiling o'er the tide:
Yet memory, like a miser o'er his store,
   Lingers with ecstasy, nor turns aside
One moment from the fascinating spell,—
Sweet sunbeam of my heart, farewell! farewell!

No. 36.

STANZAS.

"He found a flower on the prairies and he plucked it."—
THE PRAIRIE.

I.

As when some weary wanderer strays
   By pathways full of weeds o'ergrown,
And finds, far in the woodland's maze
   One simple flower that blooms alone,

Which ever after seems more fair,
  More beautiful than those that rise
Blooming along the gay parterre
  The children of far sunnier skies,
So in the world's wide wilderness
  We sometimes, unexpected, see
A glorious form of loveliness,
  The worshipped star of memory!
Whose soft mild lustre shines above
  The shadows of the darkening soul,
And mingles with each dream of love
  That o'er our musings brightly stole.

II.

There is not one in his career
  Through life's long journey who has not
Fancied or found some object dear
  To feeling which is ne'er forgot;
None are so desolate and lone
  That will not sometimes turn away
To muse delightedly upon
  The lov'd scenes of a former day.
Fancy then culls the fairest flowers,
  And weaves them into one sweet wreath,
Sparkling and fresh as life's young hours
  Whose bloom and beauty never fade;
But memory, like the lingering ray
  Of sunset, kindly flings behind
The glories of the opening day
  To light and cheer the saddened mind.

No. 37.
LOST DAYS.

"The golden age never leaves the world: it exists still, and shall exist till love, health, poetry are no more, but only for the young!"—RIENZI.

I.

Ah, my lost days! when hope was young,
And feelings deep and pure had sprung
From the glad soul, like mountain streams
That gush forth in the morning beams,
Fresh, clear, and bright, bounding away
Beneath the flowery wilding spray;
But like them, too, when they divide
To mingle with the ocean's tide,
And lose themselves in the vast main,
Never to meet or mix again!

II.

Oh! say can aught on earth atone
For youth's bright visions which are flown?
Can fame or knowledge, wealth or power,
Bring back again one golden hour,
When innocence, and peace, and joy
Beamed sweetly on the happy boy?
Ere time had taught him to conceal
One sentiment with guise or veil,
But every glowing thought would rise
Like planets in the frosty skies.

III.

But, oh ! how soon the cold earth's shade
Darkens the lustre heaven had made!
And thoughts, and hopes, and feelings fall
Back on the heart like drops of gall,
As o'er the long, long bead of days
We turn our melancholy gaze,
And there behold, tomb after tomb,
Of buried years rise, through the gloom,
And ghosts of former pleasures glide
In bitter mockery by our side.

IV.

When soft effulgence lights the way,
How easy 'tis to go astray !
Unheededly we wander on
Till life's enchanted dream is gone ;
And then where'er we turn our eyes,
All that delighted fades or flies,
Like to the baseless rainbow's dyes
Which melt into the weeping skies,
Leaving no trace or track to tell
Where all its glorious radiance fell !

No. 38.

I HAD ONE FRIEND.

I.

I HAD *one* friend in early years,
    And only one congenial mind,
Who entered into hopes and fears,
    And plans our ardent passions twined
With all those rainbow-tints which play
    So brightly round the youthful heart,
But all those visions passed away,
    And with them too he did depart.

II.

Yet like those tracks the fairies trace
    When dancing round their favourite well,
Years, pleasures, friends can ne'er efface
    The name of him I lov'd so well.
For what the sun is to the earth,
    And what the flower is to the tree,
What woman's to th' domestic hearth
    Such was my young lost friend to me.

III.

Oh, sweet as is the fragrant thorn
    When decked with pearly drops of dew,
Pure as the breath of early morn,
    And as the stock-dove fond and true,

Was he my first, best, early friend,
  Whom not a world could change or chill,
Secure him *once*, and nought could bend,
  Through every change was changeless still.

IV.

A nameless charm around him twined,
  A somthing which we scarce can tell,
An innate purity of mind,
  A voice whose accents ever fell
Softly and soothingly upon
  The lonely heart; and then there stole
Through all his kindling features one
  Bright emanation of the soul.

V.

Since then I've often sought among
  Many companions for some trace
Of kind affections, warm and strong
  Such as was ever on *his* face;
And though I've found some two or three
  Friends who still merit that dear name,
O THOMAS! there is none like thee,
  None e'er can be to me the same.

VI.

We met when the fresh heart flowed o'er
  With young affections warm and wild,
And lavished all its rich, pure store
  With the excesses of a child;

Nor thought we half enough could give,
 Since giving gave such sweet delight,
Oh! it was happiness to live
 One moment in such glorious light!

VII.

'Tis long since then, years passed away,
 And all except their memory fled;
But ever since that gloomy day
 We laid him with the silent dead,
I feel as if the world got dim,
 And light and joy forsook my breast—
For all took their bright hues from him
 Who's sunk into eternal rest.

No. 39.
AN EVENING THOUGHT.

I.

OH! how soft the evening fell,
Over rock, and hill, and dell,
 Shedding upon tree and flower
 The sweet magic of that hour
 When the heart yields to its power,
And the wounded spirit flies
To its home beyond the skies!

II.

Oh ! 'tis then our thoughts fly back
To that long-forgotten track
  Of life's pure and virtuous day
  Tracing out the tangled way,—
  Exiles seeking the lost bay,
Where they hope for succour given
To their prayers by pitying heaven !

No. 40

TO MIRZA.

With a present of early Flowers.
14th February.

I.

I WILL not send that foolish thing,
  A heartless valentine !
No ; but the heart's pure offering,
With the first simple flowers of spring :
These are the little gifts I bring—
  How long will they be thine ?

II.

The flowers, I know, will soon decay
And then be cast aside;
The proffered heart!—what dost thou say?
Shall it as quickly pass away
As bubbles in the summer-ray
   That burst as they divide.

III.

Ah, yes, I feel that fate has cast
   Our destinies apart;
If *love* can only gild the past,
Why surely *friendship* still may last
Without one rude or unkind blast
   To wound the flexile heart.

IV.

Ah, who could sigh for suns more bright
   When, looking in the sky,
We see the glorious orb of night
Climbing up heaven's star-gemmed height?
Thus, never is love's magic might
   Missed, where thy form is nigh!

No. 41.
MAID OF ERIN.

"Maid of Athens ere we part
  Give, oh! give me back my heart.—BYRON.

I.

MAID of Erin, ere we part,
Fair and lovely as thou art,

Empress of this throbbing breast,
From thee never finding rest,
Speak one word before we part,—
Wilt thou, canst thou take this heart?

II.

Maid of Erin, hear me tell,
Mingled with my wild farewell,
What my heart so long hath felt,
Where thy image long hath dwelt,
And where every thought of thee
Lives enshrined eternally.

III.

Maid of Erin, ere yon moon
Fades into soft twilight gloom
I shall be far on the sea—
Will your thoughts then follow me?
Canst thou waft one sigh to say,
"I am thine, go not away!"

IV.

Maid of Erin, that sweet smile,
Soft as sunshine o'er our isle,
Sheds a halo round my soul
Which in vain I would control;
Sigh not then, for that sweet smile
Chains me to our own lov'd isle!

No. 42.

LINES

On burning a package of letters.

" Letters have souls: they have in them all that force which expresses the transport of the heart; they have all the fire of the passions."—Letters of Eloise to Abelard, quoted by ZIMMERMAN.

I.

BLAZE on, devouring flame! nor leave behind
  A single trace of those bright " gems of thought,"
Which shine like falling stars from out the mind
  In words that seem with their own essence fraught;
A galaxy of feelings, pure, refined,
  As they were on the burning passions caught.
Ere earth could dim, or time himself impart
His chilly lessons to the glowing heart.

II.

Wreathe round the whole, enshrine them in thy blaze,
For never had the Hindoo's funereal pyre
In all the glory of its palmiest days,
  More precious things to feed the funeral fire:
Thoughts, feelings, passions, things by which we gaze
  Into the soul's pure depths, th' electric fire
Which sends a thrill into young hearts, and binds,
In one bright link of love, our hearts and minds.

III.

Oh! they were once most precious to this soul,
    As they are still most beautiful; but gone
Is all that soft ethereal light, which stole,
    Like gleams of glory shining down upon
Some spirits' isle, but fading when the whole
    Was most enchanting, and not leaving one
Lone trace of pristine splendour, but all dead,
The very life, the soul, the feeling fled.

IV.

They ceased to shine as beacon-lights of love,
    As stars which guide along the stormy way;
But, like the wrecker's brand, which flames above
    To lure the bark into some rocky bay,
They threw across my path a light to move,
    To dazzle with its beams, to lead astray,
And then to set forever from my view
When they were sweetest, and, I thought, most true.

V.

And yet it was not cold deceit was there,
    'Twas not hypocrisy, but fickleness;
The heart while it dictated was sincere,
    Sincere; too, when it felt not love's excess.
Methinks I'd feel less deeply if it were
    Not half so true in either. There is less
Regret in being deceived, than e'en to find
We had outlived the love of heart and mind.

VI.

Enough! 'tis time that with all beauteous things
  These too should pass away: pass with the flowers,
The dewdrop, and the hues which evening flings
  Along the western clouds, the moonlight hours,
And the soft melody of birds which springs
  From the recesses of the listening bowers;
Go, pass away like these, leave not a trace,
Save in this heart, which death shall scarce efface.

No. 43.

ADDITIONAL STANZAS.

Written the next day.

VII.

I'LL now get sense—I will, depend upon it;—
  And every one that knows me says 'tis time;
I'll fall in love no more with cloak or bonnet,
  I'll give up writing any more in rhyme,
Excepting now and then a little sonnet,
  For really I don't think that a great crime;
But believe me, from this day, I'll change my plan,
And be a very altered sort of man.

VIII.

I'll give up all the ladies—lips and eyes;
   I'll be no more caught with a pretty smile;
I'll set my face against all sorts of sighs
   From the real love-one to the coquet's wile.
So now, I think, already I've got wise:
   Oh! then, what shall I be when I'm a while
At this new business? Why, Solomon
Was not so wise, though somewhat greater man!

IX.

Love was the bubble that had led me on
   Through life's dark, devious ways, and when one burst
Another rose, and when that too was gone,
   Another, and another, like the first,
Appeared upon the flood, and brightly shone:
   In fact I might say that it was love that nursed
The flame of poetry from first to last
And threw its spell around me—but 'tis past.

X.

Thank Goodness, yes! and I at length have woke,
   Not like a giant just refreshed from wine;
For, take my word for it, it is no joke
   To sit and sigh in solitude, to pine
'Twixt hope and fear—oh, 'tis a heavy yoke!
   All those who call such feelings half-divine
Know very little, I am sure, about it,
And that they ever were in love, I doubt it—

XI.

At least they were not head and ears in it—
   They sounded not its depths as I have done,
Nor knelt a captive at the shrine of wit
   And beauty, until hope and heart were gone,
I know the toothache or an ague fit.
   Would be far better, though the prize was won!
So now good-bye to sighs and sentiment
And come to this scared heart, poor, common place
   content.

No. 44.

THE SEA-BOY'S GRAVE.

I.

THE moon is gone down in the blue distant wave,
To light up the amber that's strewed o'er the grave
Of the sea-boy who sleeps 'neath the foam of the billow,
Where waters wave o'er him instead of the willow,
And coral and amber are set round the pillow
   Of the sea-boy, the child of the wave.

II.

Bright sea-flowers bend o'er the place where he lies,
And murmuring waters repeat his last sighs;

And Peris of ocean watch o'er the blue deep,
While birds of the billow oft times stop to weep [56]
O'er the grave of the sea-boy who takes his last sleep
    In the foam of some sparkling cave!

III.

No tapers are lit at his funeral pile—
The moonbeam alone stole forth with a smile;
No sound save the thunders proclaimed his repose,
Yet there is one who, midst storm's and tempests arose,
And takes one fond look o'er the scene ere she goes
    To join her lost sea-boy for ever!

IV.

Yes, one whose pale, quivering figure is seen,
Like a spectre at midnight who glides o'er the green;
She wildly looks round by the moon's fitful ray,
" He calls—'tis my Dermot," she cries;—" I'll away,
Like a bright bridal robe I'll be wrapped in the spray,
    Death cannot souls like ours sever!

V.

Her bright sunny ringlets flit on the night gale,
As o'er her lost sea-boy she breathes his death wail;

Her eye raised to heaven, her heart in the sea,
Like some pagan young priestess she drops on one
    knee,
And said : "I have sworn to be constant to thee,
    My lov'd one, my husband for ever!"

VI.

Like the angel of old who used bathe in the lake,
With rapture she plunged for her dear sea-boy's
    sake :
In the white crested wave, in the deep waters blue,
Lie the maniac bride and her husband—as true
And as gentle a pair as kind Pity might view,
    Or angels conceive in their dreamings !

No. 45.
HOW OFT IN THE EVENING.

I.

How oft in the evening, when twilight appearing
    Beneath the broad brim of the sweet summer sky,
I've sat all alone, while reflections endearing
    Stole o'er me like sleep o'er the half-opened eye,
I thought of the days when I roamed through the
    wild wood,
    And plucked the sweet flowerets from the shady rill:
But these were the days, the bright days of my
    childhood,
    Though passed, yet shall mem'ry reflect them
    back still.

II.

Sweet days of my childhood, how oft you come
    stealing
  Through vistas of years o'er this once happy brow,
Like gleamings of sunshine that slowly revealing
    The scenes which past storms have made desolate
    now;
Thus mem'ry will linger o'er fond recollections
  Till, striking a chord from the ruins of time,
Whose melody, mingling with present reflections,
    Sheds o'er us a dream of enchantment sublime.

No. 46.

AN ACROSTIC.

How deep, young maiden, thy enchantments twine
Around this heart, that dares not hope for thine;
Remembrance oft shall turn her ardent gaze,
Reflecting back those few bright, happy days
I've passed with thee, unmindful of the dart
Each wingèd moment shoots into this heart!
'Twere vain, 'twere useless now, young love, to tell,
The dreams of bliss that wove this fairy spell,
Enchantress of the heart, forever fare thee well!

No. 47.
TO JOSEPHINE.

I.
I've often heard the heartless say
    That love was all a dream,
A fairy spell that glides away
    Like bubbles in a stream.

II.
I must confess that I half believed
    The story to be true;
But glad was I to be deceived,
    Josey, in meeting you.

III.
Yet some will say that woman's love
    Is sure to feel decay:
That shining first like lights above,
    Like them to fade away.

IV.
They little know how hearts like thine
    Can fondly, deeply feel—
A pilgrim kneeling at a shrine
    Feels not more love or zeal.

V.
Oh! never did young Romance throw
    Such magic o'er the hour
As when dear woman's accents low
    First owns love's sovereign power.

VI.

As that which o'er thy bosom played
    Unchangeably for years,
Like star-light that through space have strayed
    Into this vale of tears.

VII.

Though hope had sometimes nearly set
    And absence caused thee pain,
Thou hast at last thy prized one met,
    Never to part again!

No. 48.

TO ELIZA,

I.

Last evening I have watched, my love,
    Each moment still expecting thee
Until the stars shone bright above,
And even then, oh! how I strove
    To believe that thou wouldst come to me.

II.

But, no; I looked and watched in vain
    Along the path thy form to see,
Each moment adding to the pain
As hope oft went and came again,
    But still thou wouldst not come to me.

III.

And yet it was a glorious night
   As moonlight magic well could be:
A time when tender feelings might
Be breathed best in such sweet light,
   And yet thou, wouldst not come to me.

IV.

If love had settled in thy breast,
   Nay, if thou wert not wholly free,
At such a time, oh ! couldst thou rest
When heaven itself hung out its best
   Pure lamp to light thee on to me?

V.

A few days more, I know it well,
   And thou'lt be by the western sea;
But never shall love's hallowed spell
Fade from this heart. Farewell!—farewell!
   O Lizzy, sometimes think of me!

No. 49.

ON PRESENTING A FOUR-LEAFED SHAMROCK TO A BEAUTIFUL GIRL.

I.

Oh ! that it were the charmed leaf
   Which superstition fondly tells,
If it could take away all grief
   And sadness with its magic spells ;
Still, still to thee I would consign
   The fairy gift, for well I know
A kinder, purer heart than thine
   Beats not within this world below.

II.

Yet take it, for where'er thou art,
   Though it has lost its magic might,
Thy own pure innocence of heart
   Will turn the darkest grief to light ;
Thy sunny smile can chase away
   All sorrow from the suffering breast,
And thy sweet voice, with gentle sway,
   Shall make the most unhappy blest !

50.

LINES TO * * * *

Oh, my beloved, where'er I turn
Thy glances bright before me burn,
In every star that lights the sky
I see thy sparkling dove-like eye;
There's not a scented flower but brings
Back fresh to my imaginings
Deep, pure, sweet thoughts of home and
    thee,
Peri of my idolatry!
The rosebud, wet with morning dew,
Red as thy lip, and fragrant, too,
Reminds me of those smiles that came
Like sunshine o'er a flowery stream,
Flinging around where'er it fell
A magic light, bewildering spell,
A charm that twines around the heart,
Of which it forms the brightest part!
And the sweet evening's sunset glow,
Reflected on the waves below,
Seems as thy cheeks' mild, radiant, light,
Serenely pure, and mildly bright,
Where thy bright soul seems shining
    through
With glances over sweet and new:
Whate'er is beautiful or fair
Is but thyself reflected there!

SONG.

Oh! Turn again.

"That one bright look of hers, the memory of which was worth all the actual smiles of others, never left my mind."—THE EPICUREAN.

I.

OH! turn again, my lov'd one, turn
    Those looks of love and light on me,
Although their glances inly burn,
    'Twere joy to feel this pain from thee;
For like the Persians' fanes, whose fires
    Consume the altar where they blaze,
And yet, tis said that light expires
    When heaven withdraws its living rays;
So dies away the light that shone
    In sparkling radiance o'er my heart,
When those bright looks I gaze upon
    No more their former light impart!

II.

In childhood I have watched at night
    To see a star break trembling through
The twilight skies with such sweet light
    As never since hath met my view!
Years passed since then, and yet that star
    Shines in this soul just as when first
I saw its lonely light afar
    Upon my raptured senses burst;

So does that one bright look of thine
All sweet and mild and silently
Beam on through memory's cherished shrine,
And binds the heart and soul to thee!

No. 52.

LINES TO MIRZA.

"Alas! when thou hast departed from my sight, it will seem as if the moon had left the night!"—RIENZI.

ONE moment, Mirza by thy side
Is worth all other joy beside;
For thy dear presence ever threw
A spell around that none but you,
Bright lov'd enchantress as thou art
Could weave so sweetly round this heart,
And throw across life's dreary way
A light of such bewitching ray,
So pure, so bright, yet shadowy too,
Like moonbeam's glance on sparkling dew,
That never since I felt its power,
Long, long ago, up to this hour,
Has that sweet zone of gentle light
Been absent from my mind or sight!
But, like a guardian spirit's prayer,
It shone in purest radiance there,

Keeping the vast broad dome of thought,
And portals of the feelings fought
With pure affections, which to thee,
Thee only turns all doatingly!
He only who has felt Love's flame,
Kindling more bright when some dear
    name,
Is mentioned—yes, 'tis such as he
Whose heart beats most tumultuously
With deep, pure love, can only tell
The power that lives in Love's soft spell,
The strength that lies in the caress
Of Beauty's gentle helplessness!
And then how sweet, how blest to be
Near that dear object, and to see
That bright, unclouded smile which
    flings
Such light o'er our imaginings,
As summer sunset, ere he goes,
Upon the sparkling waves bestows
Where one long track of trembling
    light
Leads on till heaven and earth unite!
Oh! thus I felt, and ever feel,
Nor could not, if I would, conceal
The joy that one such moment darts
Into this very heart of hearts,

When thou art near me, pure and bright,
Like moonlight on a glorious night,
Shedding upon the earth and air
Beauty and lustre everywhere!

No. 53.

AN ACROSTIC.

Mayest thou, dear girl, be ever as thou art,
As pure in mind and innocent in heart,
Round thee may love and friendship cast their ray,
Grateful and constant as they are to-day;
Amidst life's dangers mayest thou glide along,
Rich, joyous, happy as the wild bird's song,
Endowed through life with all that nameless grace
That beams at present from thy radiant face!

No. 54.

LINES TO * * * *

I would not, oh! I could not part
With these revealings of the heart,
Though sadly painful from excess
Of deep, pure, glowing tenderness:

And throwing o'er those feelings, fraught
With love and light, a sadness caught
Within the fane, the self-same hour
I felt Love's all-absorbing power,
Like some of those old Irish airs
Enriched with sighs and gemmed with tears
Ah, no! I could not bear to part
One pang to gain a colder heart,
Or lighter feelings that ne'er knew
The charm that binds this soul to you!
Yes, I could cherish all the pain,
So that Love's flowery spell remain,
Encircling in its magic ring
All those sweet hopes young hearts can bring
Back, fresh and pure as the first hours
Of innocence, 'mid laughing flowers,
When we lov'd all we looked upon,
And earth and heaven seemed nearly one!
But break the spell or take away
The feelings I indulge to-day,
Or crush that hope that brightly stole,
Like spirits' music through the soul,
And life would henceforth be to me
A dark, unexplored wintry sea,
Without a star or guide to mark
The course of this poor shipwrecked bark!

Occasional Pieces.

No. 1.
SUNRISE.

"Where are thy beams, O sun! thou everlasting light! thou comest forth in thy beauty!"—OSSIAN.

HAIL, glorious light, before whose ray,
　Our fathers lowly bent the knee,
And welcomed in the god of day
　With songs of triumph from the free!
When first above the glittering tide
　The morning radiance did appear,
Thousands of warriors, true and tried,
　Bent low the flashing brand and spear,
And thousands turned their ardent gaze,
　In homage to the kindling East,
To catch the first pure living blaze
　From out the palace of the blest!
And *now*, though purer faith supplies
　A nobler and more sublime creed,
We still admiring turn our eyes,
　To give that glorious light its meed;

But rising still far, far above
What golden sphere though bright it be,
We turn with gratitude and love,
And give our hearts, O God, to Thee!

No. 2.

LINES

Written by Moonlight.

"It is an exquisite and beautiful thing in our nature, that when the heart is touched and softened by some tranquil happiness or affectionate feeling, the memory of the dead comes over it most powerfully and irresistibly. It would almost seem as though our better thoughts and sympathies were charms, in virtue of which the soul is enabled to hold some vague and mysterious intercourse with the spirits of those whom we dearly loved in life. Alas! how often and how long may these patient angels hover above us, waiting for the spell which is so seldom uttered and so soon forgotten."—NICHOLAS NICKELBY.

How oft I've watched that heavenly beam
When shining on my native stream,
And throwing o'er each hill and dell
The softness of its magic spell!
But never did that fairy light
Shine sweeter than it does to-night.
Oh, no! a ray more bright than this
Ne'er lit those glorious orbs of bliss,

Which now look down like angels' eyes
From their abodes of paradise !
All, all is is beautiful and grand,
Like scenery in fairyland,
Or heaven mirrored in the sea,
When all is bright tranquillity !
Oh, if departed friends have power
To wander back ! 'tis such an hour,
So full of sympathy and love,
When thoughts commune with heaven above,
And the full tide of memory rolls
In moonlight radiance o'er our souls,
Diffusing to the inmost part
The rich, fresh manner of the heart,
Until each softened thought and sense
Glows with emotions, deep, intense,
And pure, and beautiful, and bright,
As is that wavy track of light
That flings its mild and mellow ray
O'er ocean's bosom far away,
And seems to make a heavenward road
Of liquid glory unto God !

No. 3.

AN ACROSTIC.

Written (Impromptu) for a Friend on Valentine's Day.

MILDLY beams that bright blue eye
As stars that gem the midnight sky;
Rich clusters on thy forehead fair
Your simply braided dark-brown hair;
Joy, youth, and beauty weave a spell
Around thee which no tongue can tell,
No eye, no hair, no shape like thine—
Enchantress, by my valentine.

No. 4.

LINES

Written in " Childe Harold" after receiving it from a young lady to whom I had lent it.

YES, I have wandered o'er those pages bright
In secret rapture, and with more delight
Than all whose eyes *have* glanced upon this page;
Or yet may wander till, with damp and age,
Each glowing line be blotted from the sight,
And book and owner be forgot alike.

For lovely as the scenes where Byron dwells,
In dark, wild mountains, or in shaded dells,
And wild and lovely as his Ianthe's eye,
" Now brightly bold, or beautifully shy!"
Yet, oh, there's *one* whose eyes have glanced on this,
Whose fingers touched the characters I kiss,
Whose name with each fond scene shall be entwined,
Like Ianthe's name on Harold's page enshrined!

No. 5.

STANZAS

On the Very Rev. J. L. leaving Wexford.

I.

THERE are thoughts can ne'er be breathed,
    There are feelings far too strong
And too darkly, deeply shaded,
    Even to break forth in song;
But lie hid like gems of ocean
    Far below the joyous waves,
Where the stormiest commotion
    Scarcely stirs them in their caves.

II.

Thus we feel when ties are severed,
　　Which we thought would last for years,
And the fond heart still endeavoured
　　To cheat itself of its own fears;
Till the painful thought comes stealing
　　O'er the visions of the heart,
And we own with mournful feeling
　　That those links are torn apart.

III.

Ah! but yet the recollections
　　Of those ties can ne'er decay;
Deeply shrined in the affections,
　　They grow stronger day by day,
Like transparent spars descending
　　From the silent cavern's tears,
And with strength and beauty blending,
　　They get firmer still with years.

No. 6.

LINES

On visiting the sweetly romantic Valley of Brown's Castle.

I.

As some fair azure isle that seems
　　To float upon the morning billow,
And sleeping in the orient beams
　　Of which it makes its halcyon pillow;

So brightly vision-like that vale
Which burst with all its beauty o'er me,
And shines like childhood's fairy tale
Of geni-palace still before me.

II.

Sweet valley, while we lingering gaze,
    Enraptured on thy sylvan splendour,
We fear, 'twould melt in silver haze,
    So soft, so shadowy, and tender;
So full of all the heart deems fair,
    Or poet dreamt of the ideal,
That though we stand admiring there,
    We scarcely think thy beauties real.

III.

How oft, bright vale, shall memory dwell
    Upon thy streams and bowers of roses,
Where sheltered in the verdant dell,
    The still neglected loom reposes!
But, oh! if Nature's radiant smile
    Could guard it from insult and danger
It ne'er would leave our ocean isle
To seek protection from the stranger.

No. 7.

WRITTEN BY MOONLIGHT

In Ardcolm Churchyard, at the Grave of a Friend.

I.

THE moon shines sweetly on thy grassy grave,
   The stars of God are burning bright above thee,
All here is silent save the midnight wave,
   And the low voice of him who ever loved thee.

II.

When youthful friendship her enchantments threw
   Around our hearts, and hope beamed bright before thee,
I little thought the pearly midnight dew
   Would shine so soon on wild flowers blooming o'er thee.

III.

Thy gay, light heart, thy joyous laugh no more
   Will cheer the festive board where friends oft met thee,
Thy brilliant smile, thy song of love is o'er,
   But who that knew thee once could e'er forget thee?

IV.

Though years roll on, thy memory shall rest,
  Green as the grass that coldly now enfolds thee,
Thou wert a meteor of the shining past,
  Too bright to fade though life no more beholds thee.

No. 8.
WRITTEN AFTER VISITING THE GRAVE OF ROSALOO.

"He sparkled, exhaled, and went to heaven,
  The first departed of the band."—
                                CORMAC ULLA.

I.

THE lily in its brightness,
  When wet with shining dew,
The harebell in its lightness,
  The violet's star-like blue;
The sunshine in the morning,
  The silent moon at night,
All that this world's adorning
  With fragrance, beauty, light;
All that is purest, sweetest,
  And ever fresh and new,
All that is brightest, fleetest,
  Are like young "Rosaloo."

II.

There's not a bird that's singing
  Upon the wilding spray,
There's not a flower that's springing
  Upon the grassy lea,
There's not a star that's lending
  Its lamp above the wave,
There's not a voice that's blending
  The joyous with the grave,
There's not an accent falling
  From lips that's guileless, true,
But thy presence is recalling
  Young poet, "Rosaloo."

III.

And like a sunbeam straying
  To some cold, lonely isle,
Was thy pure spirit playing,
  In this dark world awhile,
And gently shedding o'er us
  Hope, happiness, and love,
'Till thou didst fade before us,
  To shine in heaven above!
And when celestial voices
  Are singing praises new,
One poet-saint rejoices,
  Young gentle "Rosaloo."

No. 9.
A TRIBUTE
To the Memory of " Donald of Shielmaliere."[57]

OH! slowly touch the clairsearch's strings,
   And sad and solemn be its strain,
For he who knew its secret springs
   Can never wake its tones again.
Yes, he, the gifted child of song,
   Whose voice first raised the tuneful band,
And pour'd resistlessly along
   Sweet notes of love and fatherland,
Has in his latest moments flung
   A glorious halo round his breast,
And, like the fabled Phœnix, sung
   His dying song and sunk to rest.
He sunk, but 'twas like evening's ray,
   That o'er the tranquil waters cast
Unnumbered dyes, which marked the way
   In bright effulgence to the last.
'Twas here among those pages first [58]
   He worshipped at the Muses' shrine,
And pour'd in one inspiring burst
   Of melody each glowing line;
Nor time, nor distance, nor yet fame
   Could e'er efface those first fresh hours,
But like a pilgrim still he came,
   With offerings of immortal flowers.

But now, alas! that voice is hushed,
  The light is gone, the song is o'er,
The words that once like streamlets gushed
  From their pure fount is heard no more;
No more his sweet-toned lyre shall wake
  The echoes of Cool-Erin's shades,
Nor e'er again their silence break,
  With love-songs for his "Moorland Maids."
No more by Oenvarra's wave,
  Nor by Temora's mouldering shrines,
No more beside the giant's grave,
  Or Croghan of the golden mines,[59]
Shall minstrels, who delighted hung
  Upon his accents, ever hear
The harp that lies untuned, unstrung,
  Of "DONALD," child or Shielmaliere.
Here let me now one chaplet weave,
  Entwining his immortal name,
And place it on the fresh green grave
  Which SHEMUS made by Tolka's stream.

No. 10.

STANZAS

Affectionately inscribed to " Glenalvon." [60]

I.

I PLUCKED a flower on a summer's morn.
'Twas glorious June; the sky, the fields, the air
Were sparkling with sweet things all heaven-born
  And beautiful;—the birds were all at prayer,
Chanting their songs from tree and sweet white-thorn;
The poetry of earth and heaven was there,
Speaking a blissful language to the heart
In characters too bright e'er to depart.

II.

There they are still reflected, true and bright,
  As are the hills along the Slaney's side,
In its blue depths, or as the stars of night,
  Making another heaven in its tide!
Oh! never can a morn bring such delight
  Again to me. Nothing can e'er divide
Or take away that loveliness which shines
  Within this soul, like gems in Indian mines.

III

Yes, there are memories that never die;
  And feelings that can ne'er recur again;
Like some rich work of genius—the last tie,
  And only trace of Eden that remain!

Whose likeness never can delight the eye,
   Or glad the heart. Oh! there is ever pain
Mixed up with pleasure, and the brightest thing,
However pure, some shadow with them bring.

IV.

Such was the morning, such its sovereign power
   Over this soul; and, willing to possess
Some portion of that beauty, one sweet flower
   Sparkling with dew, hung down in loveliness;
I plucked it! radiant as youth's virtuous hour,
   To-day I found it! oh, but who could guess
It was the same? Scent, colour, beauties fled,
Like feelings crushed, and young hopes cold and dead.

V.

'Tis ever thus, Glenalvon, day by day,
   The heart's long-cherished flowers droop and die,
Each morrow takes some lovely thing away,
   Like dewdrops that return to the sky
Just as they sparkled on the wilding spray,
   Leaving its opening petals shrunk and dry.
Oh! may *thy* heart for many years retain
The sweets of poesy without the pain!

No. 11.

TO A FRIEND, ON HIS LEAVING THE COUNTRY.

I.

How oft when mild evening in beauty is throwing
    A gorgeous farewell o'er the scene far and wide,
And when sunset in all its soft splendour is glowing,
    In circlets of gold o'er the Slaney's blue tide,
Shall I think, as I gaze on that varying splendour,
    Of the hours I have passed with the friend of my soul,
Whose heart is as warm, and whose feelings as tender,
    As e'er met in friendship and smiles round the bowl.

II.

Ah, yes! and when melody, music, and gladness
    Encircle the board at the festival cheer,
Will a thought of thee throw o'er this bosom a sadness
    When I look round and find that thou too art not here;
Like the memory of childhood that o'er us comes stealing,
    In visions too bright for the pen to impart,
Shall thy name be embalmed in the innermost feeling,
    Of all that is prized and endeared to this heart.

III.

When around thee domestic enchantments are twining,
And thy favourite boy by thy knee is at play,
And the moon in its holiest radiance is shining,
  Oh! wilt thou remember thy friend far away?
And when 'midst life's heartlessness, strife, and commotion,
  Thy heart may then turn, as turn it will,
To thy own native vales by the side of the ocean,
  Then think of one friend that is true to thee still.

No. 12.

MY OLD COMPANIONS.

I.

My old companions! how I love the few
  That still remain of all that little band!
Unlike the rest of mankind, they were true,
  And changed not; though some sought a foreign strand,
And held but slight communion with the land
  That gave them birth, yet their day-dreams stray,
And conjure up, like an enchanter's wand,
  The friends of youth, the old familiar play,
    And all those visions of life's fair but fleeting day.

II.

Yes; I have ever loved them, for they came
   And went away like the fresh flowers of Spring,
And what though- others come! they're not the same,
   Round which our young affections used to cling.
Though kind and faithful, they can never bring
   Back to the lonely heart the glorious hours
Of early life, unmixed, without a sting,
   When every scene appeared like love's own bowers,
   And all the fragrant earth one wilderness of flowers.

III.

One sought a home where evening, soft and mild,
   Threw its rich splendour o'er the western wave,
A denizen—a pilgrim of the wild,
   In foreign climes, rather than be a slave
In his own land! Oh! he was noble, brave,
   And generous; and gladly would have sought
His country's freedom in a bloody grave:
   For from his early years his spirit caught
   The light of liberty, unconquered and unbought.

IV.

Another grappled with his adverse lot,
   Until each hope and light had one by one
Faded away, and left a dreary blot,
   A stain, a mildew on a soul that shone

Amid the gloom, like lightning's flash upon
   Some splendid ruin, scathed, rent, and bare,
Fit emblem of a soul that's blasted by despair!

V.

Lowered and sunk he too hath left his home,
   A blank within his heart, and on his brow,
Not grief, nor hate, nor scorn, but each did come
   And "set his signet there," yet could not bow
Nor break that iron soul. But even now,
   As when the waters of life's summer stream
In gladness broke beneath the bounding prow,
   Oh! speak of some remembered place or name,
   And once again that soul's all love, and light, and flame.

VI.

The next is passing life away within
   A city's precincts, with its crowd and noise,
But oft his thoughts have wandered to the glen
   Where we have strayed when we were careless boys;
Aye, and that reverie gives sweeter joys
   Than the gay revels laugh of heartlessness:
The practised smile, the sparkling bowl soon cloys,
   And mirth that mocks the inward soul's distress,
   And simoon-like, makes the poor heart a wilderness.

VII.

Another sheds upon his country's page
  The light and lustre of his brilliant mind;
Now charming youth, and now instructing age,
  Awakening hope, and loos'ning bonds that bind
His country's energies that slept behind
  The clouds of passion, prejudice, and crime.
Oh! it was friends and youthful days that twined
  Themselves around his heart, despite of time,
  And flashed from out that soul thoughts brilliant, deep, sublime!

VIII.

And some are dead, and all are far away!
  Still memory shrines them in her inmost soul;
There, fresh and bright, they suffer no decay,
  But changeless, seem as when around the bowl
We met, ere time had taught us to control
  One ardent wish, or chill the glowing mind;
Yes; constant as the needle to the pole,
  Our young affections turn them, pure, refined,
  To days of early youth, and friends we've left behind.

No 13.

LINES

On Temperance.

I.

HAIL, glorious Temperance, thy blissful smile
Beams brightly still upon our ocean isle,
And gathers into one resistless band
The good, the true, the virtuous of the land.
Though storms assail, and darkness, and despair,
Hung out their murky banners in the air;
Though hope scarce sheds one ray, unless to show
The depth, the utter wretchedness of woe
Of the "doomed island," and then quickly flies,
But leaves revealed a nation's agonies!
Still, still above the darkness and despair,
One star of beauty brightly burns there,
One cherished ray that yet the storm defies,
Irradiates earth, and points unto the skies!
O Temperance! green oasis of the heart,
Handmaid of virtue, friend of every art,
Peace, piety, contentment, cheerful health,
These are thy gems that all the world's wealth
Could never purchase, these thy gifts sublime
Which fail nor fade not, but improve with time!
And *Wexford*, foremost in the glorious race,
Was first to clasp thee in a fond embrace;

Here glorious MATHEW crushed the hydra-foe,
Intemperance, rapine, wretchedness, and woe;
And still cheered on by those who love thee best,
High towards the heavens thou bearest thy flashing
    crest,
Which all that ever brilliant fancy told,
Of silver blossoms, and of fruits of gold,
Are really thine, thrice blessed Temperance,
The poor man's guide, his hope, inheritance!

No. 14.

LINES

Written after an Evening's Walk in Summer.

I.

THE sun has just gone down, how sweet this hour!
    How calm! how beautifully soft! a time
When tender thoughts, and fancy's dream have
    power
    Over young hearts, unspeakable. When chime
The cymbals of the soul with each bright flower,
    That sighs itself away. Ah, where a crime,
So great as not to feel in such an hour as this,
When earth and heaven are blending into bliss!

II.

See what a rosy halo lingers there
  Among the clouds! as if young Nature "blushed
At her own loveliness:" all, all is fair,
  And bright, and beautiful in heaven. And hushed
Are all those stormy passions fraught with care
  And strife on earth. Man's heart alone seems crushed,
Like to a dying rosebud left to pine
On its own tree, while flowers around it twine.

III.

Still 'tis the poet's hour, when his soul
  Drinks up ethereal drafts of pure delight,
More richly luxurious than that starred bowl
  Of Houris' nectar drawn from fonts of light
For warrior chiefs. Then plays without control
  That lambient flame which cheered him through the night,
When no lov'd beacon cast its guiding ray,
But shoals and quicksands strew the rocky way!

IV.

Then through the twilight of the soul we gaze
  At what we were when love and life were young;
And feelings deep and pure first caught the blaze
  Of beauty's eye, when first of love we sung,

When joy fresh sparkled through the crystal vase
   Of hope; and smiles, like moonlight, softly flung
Their angel-robes around the altar shrine,
Though broken now, yet once was half divine!

V.

Yes; broken now! where many a priestess bright
   Had fed the pristine flame; but now, ah! now,
No star of beauty sheds its hallowed light
   On the deep midnight of the scathed brow;
For storms hath gathered there in all their might,
   And billows tossed the bark of life, whose prow
Was sadly shattered, while the wished-for bay
Rose like a paradise before the way.

VI.

But rose in vain; for all the breathing bliss
   Which fancy robed creation with was gone,
And left a dark and dreary wilderness
   Of thought behind. For as we still sail on,
The waves of time, we gain at best but this,
   To know the things we prized had one by one
Passed off like stars that glimmer while they set,
Still shining on to heighten our regret.

VII.

And this is life? to see young hopes depart,
   To feel the romance of our youth decay,
And all its magic fading from the heart;
   To find the world less beautiful to-day

Than what it was before we took a part
    In its affairs. And yet it is as gay,
And fair, and faithful as when first we gave
Our hearts away—nor thought it could deceive.

VIII.

The change is in ourselves! in vain we sought
    To satisfy the soul with earthly joy;
The world's bright maze of pleasure may have caught
    The feelings of the inexperienced boy;
But soon a change will come, a serious thought
    Will fasten on the heart, perhaps annoy,
Until at length we learn that God has given
Us souls that's satisfied with nought but heaven.

No. 15.

TO R. R. WATERFORD.

On presenting him with a Copy of my Poems.

I.

You've asked me oft to send these thoughts
    I've penned in many an idle hour;
But, ah! they show so many faults,
    They prove poetry's past my power.

II.

What matter! right or wrong, here goes,
　'Tis too late now to make them better
I'll write no more except in prose
　Uncramp'd by metre, line, or fetter.

III.

It is not thus I seek to raise
　A name by many tongues admired,
Alike to me is blame or praise,
　In truth of poetry I'm tired.

IV.

Yet if among them all you find,
　A single thought to " memory dear,"
One that will still more closely bind
　The friendship that is centred here.

V.

Then I am done; I ask no more,
　My muse is getting faint and tired;
Of scribbling now I will give o'er,
　Whether degraded or admired.

VI.

I once could write a line or too
   To please myself, perhaps another;
But now, indeed, they are so few
   And bad, that I won't try *another*.

No. 16.

TO A YOUNG OAK,

Which I planted in February, 1848.

I.

YOUNG OAK, thou'rt in thy infancy
A little tiny tree,
The mildest zephyr shakes thee now,
The robin bends thy bough!

II.

But one day thou wilt proudly rise
With pride in yonder skies,
And brave the bursting thunder's wrath
And lightning's flaming path.

III.

And when the sultry summer's beams
Drink up the limpid streams,
Thy spreading boughs a cool retreat
Will give to weary feet.

IV.

And the sweet songsters of the air
Too will be there;
And beauty, love, and song will be
Thy visitants, oak-tree.

V.

But years on years must roll away
Ere thou canst see that day,
And many a glowing heart grow cold—
The youngest shall get old.

VI.

The silvery head shall then be gone,
And many a lovely one
That revels now in youth and mirth
Shall be in the cold earth.

VII.

And I, oh! shall I still be here
A wanderer in this lower sphere?
Or shall my earthly course be run
Whate'er, O Lord, "thy will be done."

No. 18.

ON THE DEATH OF MRS. C.

" Thy will be done on earth as it is in heaven."

I.

As water from some secret source
   That flows unseen through desert ground
Refreshes in its silent course
   Each drooping flower that blooms around,
So did her pure and pious mind
   Around a holy influence cast,
And in one link of sweetness bind
   Each radiant virtue to the last.

II.

Such never die, they only sleep
   To wake in glorious realms above,
Where heart ne'er sighs, nor eyes ne'er weep,
   But all is peace, and joy, and love;
Thus, like the dewdrop on the rose,
   Left by the tears of pensive even,
When daylight its first beams disclose,
   She disappears to shine in heaven!

No. 19.
ON THE DEATH OF AN INTERESTING INFANT.

    Oh! ever thus from childhood's hour
       I've seen my fondest hopes decay
    I never lov'd a tree or flower
       But 'twas the first to fade away,
    I never nursed a dear gazelle,
       To glad me with its soft black eye,
    But when it came to know me well,
       And love me, it was sure to die.
                  LALLA ROOKH.

LIKE some bright seraph that had strayed
    From his own shining realms above
To earth's fair bowers where he played
    Until he gained our hearts of love,
And left a circlet round the soul,
    Which grew intenser day by day,
And then in smiles of sadness stole
    Like moonlight from our sight away.
So ANNA ELIZA glided by,
    Making life's pathway bright and fair
As summer's dawn in eastern sky
    When heaven itself seems shining there.
Though years may pass thou'lt be enshrined
    Still in the heart's most deep recess
With all those beloved things that twined
    Around our dreams of happiness;

Yes, there, dear babe, thou'lt calmly rest,
In deep affection's holy light,
'Till in the regions of the blest
Each lov'd one shall again unite!

No. 20.

TO LIZZY IN HEAVEN.

On a beautiful and interesting child of a friend of the author's who died at the age of 3 years.

I.

Lizzy, thou art gone away,
Nothing here was worth thy stay;
Earth, though bright and fair it be,
Had no offering worthy thee.
And now, robed in rays of light,
Sunshine here seems as the night
To the blissful new abode,
Where the shadow of thy God
O'er thee throws a living blaze
Of divine, undying rays!
Lovely child, thou'rt gone away,
Nothing here was worth thy stay.

II.

Like that frail and fragile flower,
The bright lily of an hour,
Thou didst ope thy brilliant eye
To give us one sweet glance and die!
Thy young spirit didst take wing
With the first pure breath of spring,
Wafted by ambrosial gales
To those lov'd celestial vales,
Where not grief, nor tears, nor pain
Ever can be thine again!
Lovely child, thou'rt gone away,
Nothing here was worth thy stay!

III.

Little cherub, ere a shade
Of this cold earth o'er thee strayed,
Ere one hue that heaven lent,
In the place of banishment,
Was obscured by earthly ties,
Thou didst seek thy native skies,
Like the liquid pearl that gleams
In the summer morning's beams,
And exhales in fragrant air;
While we gaze admiring there,
Cherub child, thou'rt gone away,
Nothing here was worth thy stay!

No. 21.

THE POET'S SOUL.

I.

The Poet's soul is always sad
   His purest joy is woe,
He ever dwells upon the past
   And lets the present go.

II.

He sighs for other days and times
   That passed with the old year,
And makes the theme of all his rhymes
   A sigh if not a tear.

New Year's Night.

Miscellaneous Pieces.

No. 1.

THE AFRICAN WILDERNESS.

"As soon as the people of the village were gone to sleep (the moon shining brightly) we set out. The stillness of the air, the howling of the wild beasts, and the deep solitude of the wilderness, made the scene solemn and impressive. Not a word was spoken by any of us, but in a whisper; all were attentive, and everyone anxious to show his sagacity by pointing out the wolves and hyenas as they glided, like shadows in the moonlight, from one thicket to another."—PARK'S TRAVELS.

NIGHT in the wilderness!—Afric night! —
The broad moon pouring down her floods of light,
Not as she does in our cold northern isle,
Where clouds and vapour oft obscure her smile,
Not as with us, giving a feeble ray,
But rolling on in her clear, cloudless way,
Not far among the stars obscurely bright,
But almost touching her own mountain's height,
Above the tranquil glory and beneath

The loneliness and solitude of death,
Save where the wolf's and fierce hyena's cry
O'er the lone scene in startling echoes die:
A vast wild waste, far as the eye can see,
Extending like a vague eternity;
So bright, so clear though indistinct, it seems
A boundless region in the land of dreams,
A phantom country that would melt away
With the first glimpses of the break of day,
So much unlike the common things of earth,
It looks the offspring of a Peri's birth!
Strange, varied shapes each moment there appear,
And sights and sounds which make the bravest fear.
Wild, savage beasts prowl nightly for their prey,
" And savage men, as fierce, and wild as they:"
A moral desert of the human mind,
Men without aught but shape of human kind!
Where reason scarcely gives a transient spark,
But all is one wild blank, eclipsed and dark.
How fallen, how altered from a former day,
When infant Science shed her golden ray
O'er marble cities, where her footprints stand
The blasted glories of this ancient land!
Ere Greece or Rome emerged from barbarous night
Memphis and Thebes blazed forth in brilliant light,
But *War* and *Time* have shorn them of their beams
Like desert sands that drink up summer streams;
And Carthage, once the mistress of the wave,
Nor wealth, nor almost boundless power could save;

No ruined arch nor lonely colonnade
To mark the spot where she had raised her head !
Not in the fragment of a tomb to tell
Where the proud Queen of wave and commerce fell ;
But 'midst still desolation's wide domains,
O'er the scorched wilderness of Afric's plains,
Where mortal foot hath ne'er or rarely been,
There lives a power, felt, although unseen :
Amid that silent, lifeless loneliness
Man finds his hold on earth becoming less,
He feels himself a lingerer on the road
And the poor exiled soul flies to its God !

No 2.

TO RAYMOND OF FORTH, A BROTHER BARD.

Christmas Night.

I.

THE Christmas block is burning,
   Raymond dear,
And night is fast returning,
   Raymond dear ;
A star or two is stealing
Through yonder sky, revealing
The twilight hour of feeling,
   Raymond dear.

II.

Old Christmas Day is dying,
        Raymond dear,
The evening breeze is sighing,
        Raymond dear ;
And cold gray clouds are sweeping
Across the sky and keeping
The leafless boughs all weeping,
        Raymond dear.

III.

Still one bright ray is glowing,
        Raymond dear,
But while I write, 'tis going,
        Raymond dear,
And now 'tis gone, 'tis faded
Like eyes that death hath shaded,—
In starlight haze all's wreathed,
        Raymond dear.

IV.

Yet, 'tis the poet's hour,
        Raymond dear,
Richer than queenly dower,
        Raymond dear;
For thoughts on thoughts come swelling,
From the soul's deep secret dwelling,
Far, far too big for telling,
        Raymond dear,

V.

Then early dreams come o'er us,
      Raymond dear,
And old times shine before us,
      Raymond dear,
When, with spirits light and airy,
We played like woodland fairy
Without being ever weary,
      Raymond dear.

VI.

Playmates again caress us,
      Raymond dear,
And old friends once more bless us,
      Raymond dear;
The absent take their places,
The old smile on their faces,
Which e'en death ne'er effaces,
      Raymond dear.

VII.

Ah, but these times were splendid,
      Raymond dear,
Alas! that they are ended,
      Raymond dear,
Now darkness, clouds, and storms
Shut out those radiant forms,
Yet to *think* my bosom warms
      Raymond dear.

VIII.

Ay, to think, to dream for hours,
    Raymond dear,
Long passed like summer flowers,
    Raymond dear;
To coax once more around me
Each friend, each hope that bound me,—
Oh! many an hour thus found me,
    Raymond dear.

IX.

Until with pain awaking,
    Raymond dear,
I see the vision breaking,
    Raymond dear,
Like clouds at close of even,
That drink the hues of heaven
Until by storms riven,
    Raymond dear.

X.

Though time has cropped some flowers,
    Raymond dear,
From life's most cherished bowers,
    Raymond dear,
Yet some will bloom forever
Within the heart, and never
Can from that temple sever,
    Raymond dear.

XI.

The shrine that love once lighted,
   Raymond dear,
Can ne'er be dimmed or blighted,
   Raymond dear,
And though this soul hath smarted,
I feel as warm hearted
Now as when last we parted,
   Raymond dear.

XII.

May Poetry's sweet flowers,
   Raymond dear,
Illume thy leisure hours,
   Raymond dear;
May happiness attend ye,
And nought e'er blight or bend ye,
But angel-wings defend ye
   Raymond dear.

No. 3.

TO A. C.

An apology for not attending an Evening Party.

I.

OH! believe me, 'twas not for the want of esteem
    Or affection my absence was caused on last night ;
No, no, for your presence, like some youthful dream
    Ever gave to this heart's core its greatest delight.

II.

We have met, but not often, and yet, I allow,
    There was something so witchingly generous and kind
Ever beaming upon your intelligent brow,
    That 'twas painful to part so congenial a mind.

III.

When we met round the board, where the toast and the song
    Made the hours of enjoyment pass hurriedly by,
Oh! then, 'twas a pleasure to sit the night long,
    Till the stars were beginning to fade in the sky.

IV.

And then—but what matter about the *next* day
    While the *present* its brightness around us doth throw;
For languor's the tribute poor mortals must pay
    At the shrine of those fleeting enjoyments below.

V.

But could we be off to some region of light
  Where the sweets of enjoyment next day never cloy;
Oh! then, be assured I would ne'er miss a night,
  For this heart's but too willing such scenes to enjoy.

No. 4.

ON AN OLD HOUSE.

(*In imitation of Burns.*)

I.

Lament! lament, ye rhyming race,
I've no way now to turn my face,
    My house is down!
I've no way now to run for shelter
When rain come pouring helter skelter,
But o'er the scene I brood like "Werter."
    Goin' up and down.

II.

A little while, and not a trace
Of that low, humble dwelling-place
    Will mark the spot
Where first I trod the stage of life
And entered into war and strife
Of all things earthly, save a wife
    To bless my lot.

III.

How many pleasant hours I've spent
In that old house with more content,
      And childish joy,
Than I again can ever know,
Though blessed with all earth could bestow;
For then alike was friend and foe—
      I was a boy!

IV.

Old house! thou'rt dear to me as ever,
Though low and fallen, thy like shall never
      Be seen by me!
'Tis not in splendid halls of state,
Where mercenary vassals wait
Upon the noble, proud, and great,
      And bend the knee.—

V.

It is not there, depend upon it,
Though praised in many a verse and sonnet,
      The heart will find
That calm content which childhood knew
When life and all its joys were new,
And all our little friends were true
      And of one mind.

VI.

The world soon filters all away
Those feelings of a purer day,
   And leaves within
The blighted and the bankrupt heart
A rankling wound and ceaseless smart
That memory never shall depart,
   That seat of sin.

VII.

Then give me back my ivied home,
The hours of childhood and the roam
   Where fancy led;
For then this heart was free from care,
From sorrow and from dark despair,
While sunny smiles and joys were there
   That now are fled.

VIII.

The rosy cheek, the brightened brow,
The smile of joy, where are they now?
   Gone like bright flowers!
And what is left? For pity's sake
Ask not what a few years will make
Of hearts whose dearest thoughts awake
   To other hours.

IX.

Perhaps in long, long after times,
When glancing o'er these simple rhymes,
  I then may find
The hours which now neglected fly
Had friends as dear and joys as nigh
As those for whom I now do sigh
  With pensive mind.

No 5.

ADDITIONAL LINES.

Written twenty years after.

I.

How many dear ones, since the day
I've penned these lines, have passed away
  In twenty years;
And thus 'twill be till all are gone,
Like weary travellers journeying on
Through desert places, one by one,
  And disappears:
And he who writes this simple rhyme,
He too shall in a little time
  Be with the past,
Like some one on a foreign shore,
With all his treasure sent before,
Is waiting to be ferried o'er
  The gulf at last.

No. 6.

TO A TEAR.

I.

BRIGHT tear, that sparklest like a dewdrop shrined
   Within the petals of an opening flower,
Sweet gem of pity from a sorrowing mind,
   Oh! who can tell thy all-absorbing power,
The secret sympathy by which you bind
   The young, the gay, the thoughtless many an hour,
And shed a magic twilight o'er the soul,
Pure, undefinable, without control.

II.

All lovely things are loveliest when the heart
   Is touched with tenderness, and the deep springs,
Of their affections from their channels start,
   And flood the soul with sympathy: these things,
Bright as yon heaven, of which they form a part,
   Light up the mazes of imaginings,
And scintillating rays flash through our tears
That latent lay, unseen, unknown for years.

III.

'Tis in the darkness that the diamond's ray
   Shines out the brightest; and the stars are hid
On this side heaven all the livelong day,
   But when mild evening opes her dewy lid,

They come out one by one, the milky way,
  And Orion and the Pleiades shine amid
A million of radiant worlds in yon blue sky,
Like pearly tears that hang in Beauty's eye.

IV.

There is a sanctity in tears, a spell,
  A power which lies only in helplessness :
They are the poetry of grief, which tell
  Of the wrecked heart and wounded soul's distress,
When joy and hope sigh out a long farewell ;
  And in that dark and dreary wretchedness
They come, like moonbeams through a mossy shrine,
Lighting the ruin still with light divine!

No. 7.

PROLOGUE.

Written on New-Year's Night and spoken at the Young Men's Society Rooms before the introduction of Private Theatricals.

WHEN prostrate Nature cold and pulseless lies,
And tempests sweep along the sullen skies,
Old Christmas comes with measured step and slow,
Crowned with the icicle and robed with snow,
Proclaiming far and near in hut and hall
The time of mirth and solemn festival,
And calls the wanderers back, where'er they roam,
To meet again the dear old friends at home,

And all obey who can ;—but there are some
Whom Fate denies the privilege to come ;
Yet even these a small indulgence find :
Distance nor exile cannot chain the mind,
Which with a fond fidelity flies back,
O'er busy Memory's dark or shining track,
To distant scenes, which, like a dream of bliss,
Enraps the soul in such an hour as this !
Now at this time, when pleasure, far and wide,
Shakes perfumed blossoms down on every side,
When joy and gaiety light up each heart,
We, tyros of the stage, will bear a part
In the amusements introduced to-night,
To add, if possible, to your delight,
To raise the merry laugh, well pleased if we
Can place one rosebud on the Christmas-tree !

No. 8.

THE IDIOT BOY TO HIS WIDOWED MOTHER.

I.

WEEP not, weep not, mother, now ;
There's grief upon thy brow
That once was fair, and beautiful, and bright ;
But now, dear mother, all the living light,
That beauty which I lov'd to gaze upon
Is gone, for ever gone !
No smile now sparkles there,
But pallid grief and care,

And tears thou wouldst conceal I still can trace
Ever on that dear face.
Oh! once thou couldst smile on me,
And take me on thy knee,
And call me thy poor idiot boy,
Thine, and my father's joy!
What ailest thee, mother? Am I now less dear
To thee than when poor father last was here?—
Don't cry;—he told thee, ere he went asleep,
Don't you remember, not to fret or weep,
And yet thou didst not stop, but wept the more,
Faster and faster than thou didst before:
Yet, ever since the day
The strange men came and carried him away
Thou art so sadly changed,
From all, even from me estranged,
Thine own poor idiot child!
Oh! thou hast too often smiled
On me, dear mother, ever more
To frown;—look as you did before,
Sweet, calm, benignant, beautiful, and mild,
Like our dear Mother Mary with the Child.
Thou wilt not;—oh! that I could take
All thy grief away, though my heart should break;
I'd bear it all, poor mother, for thy sake!
They say my head is weak;—but, oh! my heart,
I'm sure, is right, since it can take a part
In suffering and in sorrow, and can feel
Another's woe;—but never could conceal

The faults of others from them, nor my own,
But speak whate'er I think, as if I were alone.
Mother, thy thoughts are far away;
Thou dost not mind a single word I say.
No look, no word, no smile,
Those dreary hours to beguile,
But that mild beaming eye
Is ever turned on vacancy.
Sure, when at night I gaze above
At the bright star of love,
It does not then resemble thee,
For it looks kindly down on me,
And seems to know how much I prize
The love light of the skies.
No matter, we shall never part:
I'll make up by the warmth of my heart
For this poor feeble head, and try,
By its affections, all things to supply!

No. 9.

THE WAIL OF THE SPIRIT OF THE CHURCHES
OF IRELAND.

A BURNING seraph winged his way
   From where the fount of life were playing,
And mournfully he looked that day
   When towards our Holy Island straying, [61]
For those lov'd shrines, whose light had shone
   Like moonbeams on a tranquil ocean,
Reflecting heaven itself upon
   The mirror of a pure devotion:

Yes, those lov'd fanes o'er which he kept
   His guardian-watch he saw in danger,
And even the bright angel wept
   To find the sacrilegious stranger
Had dared to set his blazing brand
   And bloody footsteps on those lonely
Beloved temples of the land,
   Sacred to God and heaven only.

   *   *   *   *   *   *

The moon rose o'er Saint Ibar's Isle, [62]
   And its old ruins once more lighted,
Like some lone lamp that burns awhile
   Above a form that death hath blighted.
But even then death could not break
   The holy spell that bound us there,
   Making it dearer far to share
Oppression for the lov'd one's sake
   Than life and liberty elsewhere!
But what new glory glistens o'er
The sainted isle from shore to shore!
Such sweet effulgence never came
From sun or moon's most mystic beam;—
Not the young "day-god," when he throws
   Open his glowing gates of bliss,
And takes from the sweet eastern rose
   Just as she wakes his pearly kiss;
Not the bright moon that floats above
   In the calm, clear, Italian sky
Such magic sheds on those who love
   And chose its light to wander by,

As those celestial beams which spring
From the bright seraph's glittering wing,
With light from heaven illumining
That hallow'd place, where once the sail
Of *Ibar* fluttered o'er the gale,
As oft upon the moonlight tide
His little skiff was seen to ride.

Yes, on that isle he turned his gaze,
  And the old ruins, torn and blighted,
Reminded him of other days,
  As on the sacred spot he lighted,
And seated on a mossy stone
  When all was silence, deep, profound,
In a soft, sweet, and plaintive tone
  Thus woke the echoes far around.

No. 10.

THE SERAPH'S SONG.

Give me a harp whose shattered string
  Hath never known a note of gladness,
And let me o'er thy sufferings fling,
  Dear Erin, one soft lay of sadness.
Where is thine ancient splendour gone?
  Thy temples, palaces, and sages
Have been extinguished one by one
  Amid the wreck of penal ages.
Where now thy colleges that gave
Instruction to the poor benighted

Barbarian from his British cave ?
   And, oh ! how well has he requited
In after times the generous hand
   That led him from his sterile mountains
To Erin's fruitful, teeming land
   Of verdant vales and sparkling fountains !
Silence now reigns where once the lay
   At midnight rung through each recess,
Until its cadence died away
   Along the cloisters' loneliness ;
Or, stealing through the long arcades
   Of arches, gathering as it lingers
Such sweetness as heaven only breathes
   From harp that's tuned by angel-fingers !
The abbey-ruins, which e'en yet,
Are viewed with feelings of regret,
As mournfully thy sons look back
Along the bloody, dismal track,
Since Saxon despotism found
A home in thy most holy ground,[63]
And turned those homes of peace and prayer
To desolation and despair;
Or into dens of vice and sin,
Where all was revelry within,
And blasphemy and jests abound
And songs profane are chorused round
By barbarous foemen, whose red hand
Had slain the sainted of the land ;
And yet the impious race will dare
To bend the knee, as if in prayer,

To God, though reeking with the blood
Of priest and pilgrim that hath stood
Fast by their altars, till the last,
    Last feverish throb of life was over,
And even then their looks were cast
    Still on the shrine, like a young lover
Who turns his dying gaze upon
    His own betrothed bride, who never
Deserted him, though all was gone,
    But clung to him as close as ever!
Yes, long as these old records last,
    They'll have the power of awakening
Thoughts of the bright and glorious past,
    Through which a hallow'd light is breaking
Still o'er the land, and never set,
    But burns now as bright as ever
Amid the broken shrines, which yet
    Hath worshippers which nought sever!
Here in this consecrated fane,
    Where oft I used to sit and listen
To the soft solemn matin strain,
    Just as the glowing wave would glisten
In morning light, where multitudes
    Of pilgrims from far foreign strands
Came to those blessed solitudes,
    And thence returned, like shining brands,
To their dark regions, dark no more;
    For there Religion now reposes,
Sent from Old Erin's sainted shore,
    Like zephyrs wafted over roses!

Oh! yes, even here the shrine is rent,
   The priests are dead, the altar's broken,
But thou art still a monument,
   An oracle that once hadst spoken
Truths more sublime than ever came
   From Delphis or Acropolis,
Whose names are on the lips of Fame:
   But what are they compared to this?
The shrine of fifteen hundred years,
   Though persecution long hung o'er thee,
The votaries triumphed in their tears,
   And now a nation's bows before thee!

No. 11.

THE DEPOPULATED VILLAGE.

"Be it a weakness, it deserves some praise,
  We love the play-place of our early days."—
COWPER.

"How often have I paused on every charm:
  The sheltered cot, the cultivated farm,
  The never-failing brook, the busy mill,
  The decent church that topped the neighbouring hill,
  The hawthorn bush, with seats beneath the shade,
  For talking age, and whispering lovers made."—
GOLDSMITH.

I.

I WENT to the play-place of my early days,
   By the side of my native stream,
Where Fancy often unconsciously strays,
   By the light of a bright day-dream;

And I seem once more a delighted child,
  With my playmates all full of glee,
But I mourn, as I sit by the bluebells wild,
  That such things never more can be.
I came like an exile to his native shrine,
  After years in the pagan's land,
But only to find all he deemed divine
  Uprooted by a merciless hand:
I came like a pilgrim-bird once again
  To revisit my humble cot,
But I roamed o'er the wide green fields in vain
  For a trace of that dear old spot.
And the green shady lane had disappeared
  That led to the old spring well,
And the bee-garden, too, so much revered,
  Where eve's parting sunbeams fell
With a softened ray through the woodbine's shade,
  And the broom and laburnum boughs,
But now all is one wide, shelterless glade,
  Where large stall-fed English cows
Roam over those places that memory makes
  As they were a long time ago,
Ere the curse of the heartless absentee breaks
  Honest hearts that are steeped in woe.

II.

I turned in silence and sadness away,
  'Twas no longer the home of the heart,

'Twas no longer the oasis of a former day,
  That could gladness and beauty impart.
I felt as the Afric traveller feels
  When he comes to the fountain side,
And finds, as he gasping o'er it kneels,
  That the waters are sunk and dried;
For, like him, I have passed o'er the desert wild,
  'Till the heart's early flowers are gone,
But I hoped that the place where I roamed as a child
  Would conjure them back one by one!
Like the desert-fountain, the *place* was there,
  But the springs of life had all fled;
And the young that I met had a brow of care,
  And the old—oh, the *old* were dead!

III.

Yes; I turned in silence and sadness away,
  To seek some old familiar face
That could tell me the cause of the quick decay
  Which had fallen on that quiet place;
But the village which stood on the green hill-side
  Was no longer reposing there,
And the wretched wanderers were scattered wide
  On the bleak world in dark despair!
A deep and appalling silence now reigns
  Where once round the cheerful hearth

The peasant's wild, sweet, untutored strains,
  And his joyous laugh of mirth
Told that happiness dwelt in the humble cot,
  And contentment had been his quest.
But, oh! how reversed now his wretched lot,
  And all those his heart loves best!
A chimney and old gable end appear
  Here and there 'mid the rubbish beneath,
And birds flying over them scream with fear—
  Oh! that dark place of danger and death.

IV.

I have heard of the pirates from Afric's shore,
  Who crept with a turbanded band
In the dead of the night to Baltimore,
  And with bloody and dripping brand
Had slaughtered the peaceful and happy there,
  As they rushed from their roofs of flame,
While the infidel muttered some text or prayer,
  And called upon ALLA'S name!
But *he* knew each drop was Christian gore
  Wrung from hearts of a hostile creed,
And he felt as he left the hated shore
  That the KORAN sanctioned the deed
I have read how the Saxon a banquet spread,
  Through the length of his castle hall,
Where a thousand lamps bright radiance shed
  Upon banner and trophied wall;

And golden goblets from many shrines
  Thickly studded the gorgeous feast,
And glittered with gems and rarest wines,
  To do honour to each noble guest;
And woman was there with her witching glance,
  And music with its soothing power,
And the song, and the feast, and the sprightly dance
  Were kept up the livelong hour.
But beneath this soft and flowery scene
  Lurked the poisoned shaft of the foe,
Like the serpent's form that crouches between
  Bright flowers, till he strikes the blow!
For 'mid nodding plumes and sparkling vests,
  With the softest and blandest smile,
The Saxon receives his Irish guests—
  The princes and chiefs of our isle.
But, lo! when the music was sweetest there,
  And the song told of Love's soft power,
When the heart was expanded and free from care,
  And festivity ruled the hour,
The clang of an armed band resounds
  Through the depths of those halls of light,
And a circle of flashing steel surrounds
  Each guest on that festive night.
A moment more, and the life-blood flows
  In spouting streams of gore,
And the pride of Erin, 'mid treacherous blows,
  Fall dead on the marble floor

And yet, though the tragic deed was planned,
  By a dastard and demon mind,
The victims *were not* of the Saxon's land,
  Nor were they of his kin and kind;
And he had been taught from his early days
  To hate with a deadly hate,
And to believe that the hand which unsparingly slays
  Merits most of the king and State.
I've been told that the fierce, ferocious Dane
  Devastated our lands long ago,
And gave churches and villages up to the flame;
  And caused torrents of blood to flow,
Round the altars' steps, in the convent cell,
  By the caves in the mountain's side;
Wherever they swept, like blasts from hell,
  All withered, and shrunk, and died.
But they deemed them usurpers that long had dwelt
  In their own magic isle of the waves,
And thought it a virtue to slay the Celt
  On the moss of their forefathers' graves!
But the infidel, Saxon, and furious Dane,
  Were not of their victims' race,
They held no intercourse with the slain,
  And but seldom saw their face.
It were those who had lived for many years
  Near the poor man's humble cot
That had quenched their fires 'mid sighs and tears,
  And drove them from that cherished spot,

To wander like sheeted ghosts above
    The graves of their buried store,
Where scarce a trace of the place they love
    Can ever cheer them more.
Ah, yes! it was he who well knew them all,
    From the time of their childhood's years,
That heartlessly over them cast a pall
    'Mid their cries, and prayers, and tears.
But he heeded not, heard not, would not let go
    His grasp on his victim's heart,
Until the last life-drops' crimson flow
    Was wrung from each suffering part.
In the eye of the law he did them no wrong,
    He could do as he liked with his own:
Here might was right, and the arm of the strong
    Was upheld by the State and throne!
Oh, was it for this God made our fair land?—
    For a mushroom aristocracy,
For the drummers of Cromwell's cut-throat band,
    And their greedy and proud progeny!

Odes of Ancient Ireland.

Ode I.

TO HEAR THE MINSTRELS ONCE MORE PLAY.

Introductory.

I.

To hear the minstrels once more play
  I've wandered far to Croghan's height;[64]
'Twas there I heard the people say
  They met in that black year of night,[65]
    To raise the wail
    O'er hill and dale,
And pour in one wild burst of grief
    The Ullaghone,
    For thousands gone—
Oh, sure it was a dismal sight!
    But since that day
    They did not play
In session held by bardic chief.

II.

And where are they, the faithful band,[66]
   The children of the harp and lyre ?
Did they forsake their native land,
   Or have they lost their wonted fire ?
      I've sought them where
      Their footsteps were,
By lonely hill and Druid's stone,
      Where once the song
      Gushed sweet along,
   And each one struck his sounding wire ;
      But now the breeze
      Sighs through the trees
With a dismal and a dying moan.

III.

Of all who woke those glorious strains
   By mountain wold or haunted vale,
Not one lone lingerer remains
   To tell his own or brother's tale !
      Yes ; there is one
      Who has not gone—
An old majestic bard is he :
      One of the few
      Bright souls still true
To Erin, who so e'er assail—
      One who still guards
      The path of bards
With spells wrought by his minstrelsy.

IV.

He stood upon his lonely hill,
   And leaned upon the "Dead Man's Chair,"[67]
As moonlight, trembling in a rill,
   Appeared his flowing beard and hair;
      But majesty
      Was in that free,
Untamed, unconquered soul, which shone
      Like mellow rays
      Of autumn days,
Dreamily bright and mildly fair!
      Retaining still,
      Through good and ill,
That light when all things else were gone!

V.

And who is he with vacant gaze,
   Lone wanderer of the heathy hill,
Whose thoughts are with long bygone days,
   And with old forms he lov'd so well?
      What brings him where
      The "Dead Man's Chair"
Frowns a dark, dreary canopy?—
      Does Ossian's form
      Ride on the storm,
Does he rise from his hall of shell?
      Ah, no!—'tis one
      Who still lives on,
'Tis he, the last old *Senachie!*[68]

VI.

And seated on a mossy stone,
  That Druid might have used of old,
The bard pours out his parting moan
  In measures musical and bold,
    That told of days
    Lost in the haze
Of long, dark years of grief and woe :
    And bright ones, too,
    When Erin slew
The Dane within his guarded hold ;
    And swept the land
    From strand to strand,
From foreign and domestic foe !

ODE II.

A PRELUDE—THE SONG OF THE LAST
SENACHIE.

I

My eyes are dim with grief and age,
  My hands are palsied, too, with care ;
My heart is torn, like Erin's page,
  And left all bleeding, bruised, and bare.
But memory still delights to gaze
  Along the half-forgotten track

Of my lov'd country's ancient days,
   And conjure all their glories back!
Then come, my harp !—give out a tone,
And let thy fiercest numbers swell,
   Let them be wild, and strong, and deep,
And burning while we strive to tell
   Of scenes that would make angels weep,
   And shame the very fiends in hell!
Yes, we shall tell them one by one,
And long, I'm sure, before we've done
   Thou'lt marvel that such hearts as ours,
   With all their high chivalric powers,
Could brook so long the burning stain
   That branded us the worst of slaves,
But would not break in bits the chain,
Or let our heart's last life-drop drain
   Upon ours, and our fathers' graves.
What is there mete from Freedom's shrine
   In all that's noble, great, and grand,
And beautiful, that is not thine ?—
   Profusely scattered o'er the land,—
Thy vales are sweet as glimpses seen
   By poets in their blissful dreams.
And what can equal Erin's green,
   Or match the brightness of her streams ?
Do not the dashing waves surround
   And guard like sentinels her strand,
Protecting it like holy ground
   From every foe and foreign hand ;

Are not her mountains' lofty crest,
  When catching the last light of even,
A nation's charter-seal impressed
  And ratified direct from heaven?
Be still, my soul—let others tell,
  How like a free-born state thou art,
While I upon thy griefs shall dwell
  Until I get them all by heart!

Ode III.

THE MILESIAN EXPEDITION TO IRELAND.

"On a fine morning in May the Milesian fleet left the Bay of Corunna, in Spain, in search of the Isle of Destiny, which their ancient prophecies declared should be their final home. After a stormy passage through the Atlantic they attempted to land on the coast of Leinster, at a place called Inbher Slainge, now known as the harbour of Wexford; but the De Danaans, who inhabited the island, by their magical enchantments, wrapped the island in a cloud, so that it appeared to the Milesians under the form of a hog."—KEATING.

THE fleet is riding in Corunna Bay:
" Prepare ere morning's dawn to be away,
Unfurl the banners, spread aloft the sail,
And woo with every sheet the passing gale;
Oh, quickly waft us far from sunny Spain,
To that bright land we dreamt of o'er the main!

Princes, the hour destined by fate at last
Has now arrived, and all our wandering's past:
That 'Sacred Island,' which our prophets told
Should be our country in the days of old,
Shines where the setting sun his farewell takes,
And lingers last upon her mountain peaks,
Divided only from us by the foam,
Which once surmounted shall become our home.
'Tis said 'tis guarded by the Danaan brood,
Men of gigantic stature, fierce and rude,
And given to plunder, rapine, force, and fraud,
They've spread the terror of their name abroad;
A land of sorcerers, whose charms swell
Around the coast like blasts raked up from hell;
But still their magic is of no avail,
Since 'tis decreed by fate that we prevail.
Unfurl the Sunburst;—let our banners free
Upon the gale that's freshening from the sea;
Let skean and spear be ready for the prey
Ere sets the glories of the God of Day,
Whose beams already, see, begin to rise
In cloudless majesty along the skies."
Thus spoke Prince Heber to the chieftain throng,
When harp and timbrel, clashing arms and song,
And deafening cheers from ship to ship arose,
Which bid defiance to their Danaan foes.
These joyous shouts had scarcely died away,
When rose their Day-God o'er the waters' bay.

Then in an instant every warrior's gaze
Was turned to catch the first bright, living rays,
And knees were bent like Arab hosts at prayer,
While lance and spear were crouched in homage there,
And golden vapours rolled along the shore
In wreaths of glory, which the breezes bore,
Like incense offered at some pagan shrine,
Whose votaries worshipped what they deemed divine.
Deep silence reigned as if some magic wand
Had turned to stone each of that warrior band,
So rigid, motionless, and fixed they gazed
At that bright spot where their young Day-God blazed,[69]
Until Amhergin, the high priest, at last,
With voice as strong and clear as trumpet blast,
Proclaimed the hour for the morning song
To all the votaries of that shining throng.
Then harp and timbrel mixed their votive strain
With warrior voices far across the main,
From ship to ship the electric spirit ran,
And one loud chorus ran from rere to van.

Ode IV.

THE MILESIANS' MORNING HYMN

To the God of Day.

I.

Oh, thou, whose bright and living ray
  Awakes the universe from sleep,
Inspire thy votaries to-day
  With courage strong and purpose deep ;
Let not a soul be wanting here
  In all this high devoted band,
To wield the flashing brand and spear,
  And die to win our destined land.

II.

There's not a gem from deepest mines,
  There's not a tree that waves on high,
There's not a flower that sweetly shines,
  But's born beneath thy radiant eye;
There's not a hill or mountain's crest,
  There's not a vale or prairie wild,
But clasps thee to its loving breast,
  And fondly greets thee like a child.

III.

The eagle in his lordly flight,
  The feathered songsters from each tree,
The condor, in his power and might,
  Pay early homage unto thee ;

The skylark poised in morning air,
  And warblers from each flowery spray,
All join in one sweet vocal prayer,
  To worship thee, young God of Day!

IV.

The beasts that through the forests sweep,
  Or crouch within their savage lair,
The creatures of the boundless deep,
  All wake and worship thee in prayer;
Shall we not, then, in grateful praise,
  Salute thee with our harps and voice,
And welcome the first living rays
  Which makes all Nature's heart rejoice.

Ode V.
THE MILESIANS SAIL FOR IRELAND.

"The fleet being provided with all things and ready to sail, the entire colony, divided into different tribes, embarked with their wives and children, their vassals and soldiers, artisans and labourers of every kind, under forty chiefs. After coasting along part of Spain, Gaul, and Britain, they at length arrived on the southern coast of the Western Island, which had been promised to them by their prophets. Whilst they were preparing to disembark, they were overtaken by a violent storm, which soon changed their hopes into despair. The heavens were darkened; a wind from the south-east swelled the waves, so that in a little time the fleet was scattered, and out of sixty ships, of which it was composed, not two of them remained together."—MAC GEOGHEGAN'S "HISTORY OF IRELAND."

WITH hearts exultant, and with souls as brave
  As e'er were wafted on the western-wave,

The fleet sped onward to the destined shore,
Each sail unfurled, every flashing oar
Like sea-gulls dipping in the crested foam,
Hastened the squadron to their long-sought home.
Full forty warriors, each a ship commands,
Men known to fame in many distant lands;
Where all are brave 'tis scarcely fair to boast,
But he who's humblest often merits most;
Where all are valiant where's the use to tell,
How Heber conquered, or how Fearon fell,
How Heremon triumphed in a hundred fights;
Or how fierce Leighne of the Red-branch Knights
A thousand times rolled back the tide of war;
Or how young Orba, like a blazing star,
Flashed through the thickest of opposing blows,
The light of battle and the dread of foes!
The evening sun had crimsoned all the west
With clouds of glory where he sinks to rest,
And yet no trace of aught save sea and sky
Did bless the sight of the most practised eye,
Whose looks were cast, without a moment's change
To where they fancied lay old Inbher Slainge.[70]
At length a vision like enchantment breaks
Through parted clouds, with many-coloured peaks,
And glens, all glowing in the setting sun,
Proclaims their wanderings now are nearly done.
"'Tis Inbher Slainge!—'tis Inbher Slainge at last!"
Pealed from each ship from deck and tapering mast.

"The Isle of Destiny before us lies—
The wanderers' home, the warrior's dearest prize!"
But soon those shouts that seemed to rend the air
Sunk into silence, for the hour for prayer
Is now announced, in accents deep and strong,
By Prince Amhergin, who, with harp and gong,
Invites the warriors to the evening song
Of praise and glory to the God of Day,
Who is brightly sinking in the waves away,
Far to the west, making a track of light,
To where the heavens and the earth unite!

Ode VI.

THE MILESIANS' EVENING HYMN
To the God of Day.

I.

HAIL, glorious light, now sinking fast
Into the depths of ocean vast,
And shedding thy mysterious beams
On Innisfail's bright hills and streams;
Thou who hast guided us since day
So safely o'er our devious way,
To thee we turn our ardent gaze,
And offer up our evening praise!

II.

Although now fading fast away,
Oh! guard us till the coming day,

And light up in our souls a flame
Unquenchable, until thy name
Triumphant shall in glory shine
Upon each hill-top, where a shrine
To thee of living fire shall blaze,
Bright as in ZOROASTER'S days! [71]

III.

How many sacred shrines to-day
Were lighted by thy kindling ray!
The cities where our fathers dwelt,
The homes where first to thee we knelt,
The countries which once bore our sway,
From Persia's plains to bright Cathay,
Their graves by many a foreign shore,
Which we can never visit more!

IV.

Though these are sweeter to us than
The flowery vales of Ispahan,
And dearer than the golden mines
Of Opher's consecrated shrines;
Yet we have left them all to roam
In search of our long-promised home,
That sacred island of the west,
Our destined place of final rest! [72]

V.

Then guard, direct, inspire us still
With light, till we our task fulfil,

And pour fresh courage in our hearts,
To triumph over Danaan arts;
And we our votive gifts shall bring
To thee of every precious thing,
And altars to thy name shall blaze
Through all the isle for endless days!

Ode VII.

THE STORM.[73]

The sun had gone down,
  Amid glory and splendour,
And eve's purple light
  Came down mellow and tender,
But mists gathered fast
  On the heights of the mountain,
And rushed down its sides
  Like an overcharged fountain;
The lightnings leaped forth
  From the black clouds that bound them,
And thunders peeled out
  'Mid the crags that surround them,
And the island they gazed on
  With looks of devotion,
Now seemed but a fog
  On the breast of the ocean!
The tempest swept on
  Over breakers and billows,
And shattered their fleet
  Like a light bark of willows,

As onward they dashed,
   Through the darkness that lowered,
Till, scattered and broken,
   They lay overpowered
By spells of enchantment
   That strongly came o'er them,
And shut out the hope
   Which for years shone before them!

*   *   *   *   *

Ode VIII.

AFTER THE STORM—THE LANDING.

I.

The spell had spent itself at break of day;
   The storm had ceased, the war of elements o'er,
But, oh! for those whose hopes were cast away!
Like surges breaking on a rocky bay!
   The signs of wreck were strewed along the shore,
And mast, and helm, and torn sail were seen
   Struggling at intervals to gain the land
In pairs or singly, with rough waves between
   The scattered fleet, now reft of all command,
Save what each single warrior brought to bear
To light up hope once more, and shut out grim
      despair!

II.

The ships were parted, some were borne away
   Through rocky islets of the western wave,
Others were driven along the Irish sea
Until they came to Inbher Colpa's Bay;[74]
   Here Heremon landed, sad, yet bold and brave
And fierce as ever sprung upon the strand,
   Unfurled the Sunburst to the morning breeze
And took possession, while each flashing brand
     Leaped forth, as warriors on their bended knees,
Raised them aloft to heaven, and fondly swore
To make their homes or graves upon the shore.

III.

The largest portion of the fleet was cast
   In whirling blasts along the rocky coast
And treacherous isles of Desmond, where at last
The valiant IR, with all his crew, were lost
   Amid the raging elements; but most
Of all the rest made Inbher Secine's shore [75]
   Where Heber and Amhergin, tempest-tost
And shattered, through the breaking billows bore
   Aloft the standard to the isle which cost
The proud Milesian so much toil and woe,
Which nerved them stronger still to meet the foe.

Ode IX.

THE FIRST BATTLE—THE MARCH.

"The landing of the Milesians took place in the year of the world 2736, according to the Hebrew computation, on the 17th day of the month of Bell, or May. The Damnonii having in the meantime, collected their forces with singular expedition, attacked Heber in his entrenchments. Heber had taken possession of his camp at Sliagh Mis, in the county of Kerry, where an obstinate engagement took place, the third day after his landing; but the superior valour of the Milesians prevailed, and the Danaans left 1,000 men killed on the field of battle. The Milesians themselves lost 300 men, two Druids, and two ladies, Scota and Fais, with some leading officers."—M'DERMOT'S "HISTORY OF IRELAND."

I.

Men of bright Migdonia's land,
Couch the lance and draw the brand,
Sound the timbrel loud and long,
Thunder forth our warriors' song;
Like the midnight tempest's roar
Breaking on a rocky shore,
Let the trumpet's fiercest sound
With our war-tramp shake the ground.

II.

Rear the holy Sunburst high
Ere our Day-God lights the sky,
Bear upon the silver throne
Jacob's consecrated stone, [76]

Which upon the Red Sea shore
Moses gave our sires of yore,
Strew the sands his footsteps trod,
Onward !—see the beams of God !

III.

Warriors ! let the glorious past
Nerve us like the bugle's blast,
Guide the arm, and point the lance,
As our shining ranks advance ;
Sweeping o'er the fallen slain
Like a whirlwind on the main,
Whilst one Danaan taints the air
Crush the brood and do not spare !

Ode X.

THE BATTLE—THE ENGAGEMENT.

O'er the broad valleys of high Slieve-na-Mis, [77]
Whose peaks are hid among the clouds they kiss,
The squadrons meet in battles' bright array
Just as the portals of the opening day
Had flung their slanting beams along the glen,
Now filled with hostile ranks of armed men,
Impatient to begin the murderous strife,
Panting with rage and prodigal of life.
The Danaans moved with caution o'er the bank,
Close and compact as serried rank on rank,

In silence formed their final enfilade,
They seemed like warriors merely on parade,
Who trusted to their necromantic charms,
To be victorious in this deed of arms.
The proud Milesians, maddened at the sight,
Dashed down the glen, impatient for the fight,
With one wild cheer that made the rocks resound,
As if an earthquake shook the solid ground.
Each takes up his position where assigned,
As if the thousands there had but one mind,
One spirit guiding, and one only care,
Pervades the shining ranks from front to rere,
To die or conquer, to succeed or fail,
To be the victors of Green Innisfail!

III.

The tumult ceased; along the extended line
Each warrior stood like a tall mountain pine,
Erect and motionless, as if some spell
From Danaan necromancy on them fell.
A dreadful silence reigned, deep and profound,
And more appalling than when o'er the ground
The hostile forces meet in deadly strife,
No thought but vengeance, and no care of life,
For then the passions all are up in arms,
Shut out all danger and despise alarms.
'Twas but a moment thus, yet seemed an age,
So eager were the forces to engage;
And when Prince *Heber* on his charger flew,
From rank to rank to stimulate anew

Their high-wrought courage, lest one craven mind
Should fail or falter, or remain behind,
There rose a booming sound, fierce, furious, fast,
Like thunders mingling with the whirlwind blast,
And banners waved, and battle-axe and brand,
And skene and spear flashed in each warrior's hand.
While lance and javelin, in early morn,
Bristled as thick as fields of bearded corn,
And targe and helmet sparkled here and there
Like lightning playing round from front to rere.

III.

As sounding avalanches downward sweep,
Resistless onwards to the valleys deep,
And crash through hanging shrubs and beetling rocks,
O'erwhelming shepherds and their frightened flocks,
So rush both armies to the dire attack,
Leaving along the plain a bloody track,
And helm and skene and javelin and targe
Are rent and shattered in the deadly charge ;
Here battle-axe broken, there a sword hilt left,
Yonder a banner torn, and helmet cleft,
And mangled limbs and headless trunks lie round,
And ghastly bodies cumber all the ground,
Trod down and trampled on by friend and foe,
No thought but who could give the fiercest blow,
And surging back and forward o'er the plain
The dying warrior drops among the slain :

Nor fears nor feels aught of his own distress,
So he could only make one foe the less.
The conflict deepens; the Milesians, led
By Prince Heber, rushed o'er lanes of dead,
While Danaan valour in the next attack
As fiercely drove the foemen reeling back.
Dubious and doubtful rolled the tide of war,
As victory slowly drove her sanguined car,
Now to the left, then slowly towards the right,
Again in front among the thickest fight,
Then noiselessly withdrawing from the field,
Where valour could not win and would not yield.

IV.

Near to the plains there rose a gentle height,
And here, secure from harm and hostile sight,
The Princess Scota, with a youthful train,
Beheld the battle field all strewed with slain,
Her bravest warriors waver, driven back
By the fierce Danaan murderous attack,
Leaving the holy Sunburst in the rere,
Their pride, their hope, their most devoted care!
Seized with despair the princess snatched a skene,
And in wild fury rushed o'er heaps of slain
To where the Sunburst fluttered still on high,
Resolved to rescue it or bravely die.
Around her gathered the young Gadeline,
Sons of the bravest princes of the line,

Cuala, fierce as a young beast of prey,
And Elbhe, brave as a wild wolf at bay,
Breas and Un, the lamp and light of war,
Young Etan, brilliant as a shooting star
And Lui, swift as the red mountain deer,
With Bladh, monarch of the sounding spear,
Neré the valiant, too, pressed close beside
Courageous Cacier, the fond hope and pride
Of all the warriors of that little band,
Though few, yet fearless as e'er grasped a brand.
These formed her guard, and round her like a shield
Flashed skene and battle-axe along the field,
Till like a magnet their fierce valour drew
Their broken ranks together to renew
The deadly combat with resistless sway,
Which swept their foes like withered leaves away
Along the plain upon a stormy day.
The Danaan force was beaten, crushed in gore,
Their valour sunk their war-note heard no more;
Yet with despairing energy they fought
Around the Sunburst, till a foeman caught
The "holy banner," that for ages led
The troops in triumph over fields of dead,
And waved victorious over sea and land,
But ne'er till now was grasped by hostile hand.
Wild shouts of triumph and deep yells of rage,
Surprise, and terror now both sides engage,
When, with the swiftness of a mountain roe,
The Princess Scota sprang upon the foe:

. Her skene flashed quickly, and the shining dart
Sank quivering deeply in the foeman's heart.
The strife was ended, and the Sunburst borne
In triumph floating on the breeze of morn,
But all was purchased at too dear a rate,
For here the fearless princess met her fate :
A broken lance that moment pierced her breast,
Which to conceal she covered with her vest,
And borne in triumph to a rising mound,
None knew she had received a deadly wound,
Until they placed her on the purple heath,
Where her eventful life was closed in death ;
There, drawing out the shaft with sparkling eyes,
She faintly faltered "Victory," and dies. [78]

Ode XI.
THE PRINCESS SCOTA'S BURIAL.

I.

THE sounds of strife had died away,
And death had seized his noblest prey,
The princess that had o'er them shed
The glories of the past lay dead ;
The royal daughter of the Nile
No more can o'er their victories smile.
Let the proud house of Pharaoh mourn
To-day upon bright Scota's urn.
A mournful train now moves along,
With cypress wreaths and solemn song

And harps whose wild and wailing tone
Told of a much-loved spirit gone.
They laid her on the green sward down,
And placed upon her brow a crown,
A golden sceptre by her side,
And robed in white like royal bride,
While bow and quiver, targe and spear,
Were placed around her grassy bier,
And everything the earth holds dear
And precious all were gathered there.
The lotus from the lordly Nile,
And Sharon's roses formed the pile;
The mystic fire from Persia's shrines
In crystal vases dimly shines,
And sand from off the Red Sea shore
Was mixed with myrrh and sprinkled o'er,
And perfumes from sweet Yemen's vale
Wafted their fragrance on the gale.

II.

They raised the tumulus in grief,
And every prince and warrior chief
Came laden with a massive stone,
And placed around her a rough zone
Of unhewn rocks, borne from the plain
On which no chisel left a stain,
But pure as from the hands of God,
They placed them round the verdant sod,
And over all, like a low dome
They placed the monumental stone,

And raised a mound of ample space,
Which centuries could not efface;
Then sad and silently each chief
Placed on the heap a stone of grief,
Until a cairn large and high
Was raised, which tells the passers-by
That there a princess lies beneath
Within the narrow house of death.
And as some strangers stray to-day
Along the lone and gloomy way,
The peasants in low whispers tell
How here a lady fought and fell,
And to record the mournful tale
They call the place Queen Scota's vale.

Ode XII.

THE DIRGE.

I.

Soft be thy slumbers here to-day,
    Oh, princess of the fearless heart!
No more thou'lt light our saddened way,
Or cheer our footsteps as they stray
    O'er mountain glen or forest deep,
    Or chase the Danaan to his keep!
    Now we can only wail and weep
Around thy tomb, while groan and tear
But faintly tell how lov'd, how dear,
    How fondly prized, revered thou art.

II.

Let Ula of the mournful string
    Pour out a dirge of plaintive sound,
And o'er our saddened senses fling
The song of grief which warriors sing
    Around the bed where valour sleeps,
    And fond affection wails and weeps
    As she her sacred vigil keeps.
Then let thy harp our sorrows tell
Before we say our last farewell
    To Princess Scota's lonely mound.

III.

Dark Ula slowly moved along,
And with him all the sons of song,
To the lone tumulus of grief,
Round which assembled prince and chief
And warriors that had never felt
What 'twas to weep, now lowly knelt,
With drooping banners trailing low,
Expressive of their heartfelt woe
That settled on that shining host,
For her whom they had loved and lost.
A thousand voices sent a wail
Of piercing sadness o'er the vale,
As Ula passed his hands along
The harp-strings and began the song.

IV.

Give out, O harp, the saddest strain
   That's sleeping in the strings;
Oh ! breathe the deepest notes of pain
   That pure affection flings
Around those hearts who find relief
In the wild luxury of grief !
Weep ! soldiers weep o'er Scota's shrine,
   Bright princess of the Nile ;
Queen of the fearless Gadeline
   We wail around thy pile,

V.

The halls of Thebes are dim to-night,
For she who shone a star of light
   Can them no more illume,
Like some bright meteors that rise
And flash along the midnight skies,
She shed a momentary ray
Around us, and then passed away
   To the dark, silent tomb.

VI.

Fair as the moon upon the hill,
Pure as the sparkling mountain rill,
   And as gentle as the dawn ;
And yet, thy heart was void of fear,
Whenever danger hovered near,
And bold and brave as the wild deer
   When guarding its lov'd fawn,

VII.

Oh ! princess of the faithful heart,
   How can we believe that thou art dead,
Too sudden came the fatal dart,
   Too quickly thy lov'd spirit fled.
Canst thou no more be our sweet guide,
   Or join us in the festive hour,
Must we no more walk by thy side,
   Or share thy pleasure, pride, or power ?—
Thou who hast led us safely on,
   O'er distant lands and oceans vast,
How can we believe that thou art gone,
   And we have looked on thee our last ?
Yes ; like the gentle, faithful dove,
   That fondly lighted on the ark,
Thou hast shed o'er us peace and love,
   Then passed away, and all was dark !

VIII.

Come, then, my children, raise the wail,
Let sights and sorrow here prevail,
Sad, mournful strains alone shall chime,
While hearts in unison keep time,
And souls sigh forth with every note,
That on the evening breezes float
Up to the clouds all fringed with gold,
Which our great forefathers unfold,

As they on misty couches lie,
And look down on us from the sky,
Like sentinels that guard the brave,
And watch with care Queen Scota's grave!

IX.

Here, then, we leave thee, while we go
Again to meet the daring foe,
And mingle in the deadly strife,
For home and country, fame and life
Till victory triumphant smile
Upon our arms, and make the isle,
Long promised to our ancient line,
The home of the proud Gadeline.
And, oh! if thou canst aid impart,
And stir up courage in the heart,
Here round thy sacred shrine we swear
That our new home thy name shall bear,
And that through all succeeding days
The people shall recount thy praise,
And as they drop a tear the while,
They'll call the country Scota's isle!

Ode XIII.

THE ENCHANTED PALACE OF THE DE DANAANS.

I.

The sun rose dreamily and bright
O'er Sliev-na-Mises' alpine height,

And all the hills and valleys round
Appeared to be enchanted ground,
So bright, yet indistinct they seem,
Like flowers mirrored in a stream,
Where each bright wavelet, as it flows,
Reflects the colour of the rose,
In soft prismatic rays, which gleam,
For ever changing, yet the same.
And far in Tailton's verdant plain
   The Danaans' magic palace shines,
Where sounds of mirth and music's strain
   Come floating through the oaks and pines;
And revelry, and joy, and song
Hold sway within the whole day long,
And birds are singing from the trees
To add to those soft melodies.
A thousand banners deck the walls,
A thousand warriors throng the halls,
And ladies, bright as forms that gleam
A moment through some youthful dream,
Glide to and fro with sweet caress
Of youth's eternal loveliness,
Which time nor age can e'er make less,
As magic spells each day renew
Their freshness with ambrosial dew.

II.

Around the portals magic guards,
   That never slumber night nor day,

Keep jealous watch, while numerous bards
  With music wile the hours away.
Enchanted statues ranged in state,
  Throughout the long arcades of light,
Wait but a touch to animate,
  And make them fiercest in the fight.
Secure in necromantic charms,
  The Danaan chieftains spend the day;
Free from all cares and war's alarms,
  They pass their dreamy lives away.
In soft, voluptuous ease some move
  Through flowery arbours' silent shades,
And breathe soft tales of ardent love
  To the young gentle Danaan maids.
Some quaff the sparkling usquebaugh,
  Others recline on thrones of state,
Pleasure their only aim and law,
  They seem beyond the reach of fate!
And yet, beneath this playful mood,
  And all this outward gentleness,
The fiercest passions oft intrude,
  And rage in all their hideousness;
Those, but the fragile flowers that grow
  Upon the mountain's heaving height,
These, the volcanic fires below,
  That blast them with their withering might!

III.

Let but a single war-note pierce
   Those festive bowers of calm repose,
And all their smouldering passions fierce
   And deadly, flash out on their foes;
Let but one hostile banner spread
   Its folds upon the morning air,
And every gentle feeling's fled,
   And all the demon soul left bare.
If footsteps of marauding foes
Came near to break their soft repose,
Or chanced to cross their guarded path,
Fearful and furious was their wrath.
Blue meteors flashed along the halls
From lamp and tripod on the walls,
And banners waved, and spear and targe
Rang out, as if a deadly charge
From unseen hands had dealt a blow
Which crushed in gore the conquered
    foe.
Statues from niche and pedestal
Sprang like so many fiends from hell,
And in their stony arms clasped
Their struggling victims, till they gasped
   Away the last faint throb of life
In deadly hatred and despair,
   Or mingled in the fearful strife
Which raged in merciless havoc there.

'Twas thus our great forefathers found
   The Danaan palace, when they stood
Before the gates, in armed array,
One morning, at the break of day,
   And dyed in gouts of the best blood
The whole of that enchanted ground.

Ode XIV.
TAILTON.

I.

'Tis night at Tailton : silence reigns around,
   The very air is hushed in soft repose,
And all is still in that enchanted ground,
   Save where the stately Danaan palace rose—
A radiant gem, where feast and festive sound
   And joyous revelry and music flows,
And dance and song hold undiminished sway,
Though night had nearly blended into day.

II.

The crescent moon shone through the cloudless night
   Robing the earth in beauty like a veil
Of silver sheen, and flooding with its light
   Each crag and cliff, each mountain-top and vale :
A time when contemplation takes a flight
   Beyond the verge of earth, and heavenward sail
Far as the electric spark of thought can soar,
   Till the enfranchised soul can bear no more.

III.

Who has not wandered forth in the calm noon
    Of a clear night, and felt a pleasing, deep
Regret, a sadness that he should so soon
    Leave that sweet light for the repose of sleep
And blank forgetfulness ?—it is a boon,
    Like glimpses of all beauteous things, which keep
Possession of the heart through good and ill,
'Midst sunshine, storms, or cold it lives there still.

IV.

'Twas such a night as this, in Tailton vale,
    The Danaan palace rang with festive song ;
Hundreds of warriors clad in glittering mail
    Mingled with ladies here and there along
The halls like phantoms of a fairy tale.
    Some joined the dancers' bright and mazy throng,
And some in magic mirrors sought to see
The dim impression of futurity.

V.

It was a princely banquet ; all the pride
    And pomp of royalty assembled there,
To grace the nuptials of a Danaan bride
    With the Dannonians' favourite prince and heir
The magic guards were ranged in groups outside,
    And spells of deep enchantments filled the air
While usquebaugh and nectar flowed around
In golden goblets through the palace ground.

VI.

But when the feast is at its height, and joy,
   And mirth and gladness filled each glowing breast,
There came a change for ever to destroy
   The peace and gladness of both host and guest.
What are those sounds the royal feast annoy?
   Why that wild wail as if from souls distressed?
Why flames the tripods' lights red, blue, and green?
Why wave the banners fierce by hands unseen!

VII.

Confusion thickens: hideous forms appear
   And glide along the banquet-halls of state,
Statues advance to grasp the brand and spear,
   While muttering voices chant the dirge of fate.
Now far away, and now fearfully near.
   Full well they know these omens, and await
Until their incantations should disclose
The force and aim of their advancing foes.

VIII.

The seer is summoned, and the spell is cast;
   High flames the cauldron in the banquet-hall.
How stands the spell? What tells that lurid blast?
   Is the Dannonian dynasty to fall?
Or is their power, still unimpaired, to last?
   Come, spirits of the deep, earth, air, and all
Open the Book of Fate, and let them see
The annals of their future destiny.

IX.

The prince of sorcerers, with charm and spell,
    And many a mystic rite moves round the blaze,
Invoking those deep shadowy shapes that dwell
    Beyond the ken of mortal, and can gaze
Into the future, to appear and tell
    The issue of the contest, and the ways
And means they should adopt to crush the foe,
And all the occult forms of Chance to know.

Ode XV.

THE SPELL.

I.

KING GREINE.

By the power of this spell,
Spirits, wheresoe'er ye dwell,
In the caverns of the deep,
Or where wild tornadoes sweep,
In the farthest realms of night,
Or within the rainbow's light,
By the mountain or the stream,
Or in flashing lightning's gleam,
In the moonlight's silvery ray,
Or the orient beams of day,
Wheresoever you may dwell,
Spirits, now obey this spell:

By this thrice enchanted spear [79]
We command you to appear!

SPIRITS' VOICES.

We are here!

KING GREINE.

There are spirits on the wing,
Hovering round this magic ring,
Something in our hearts declare
Millions of them fill the air:
We can feel that they are near;
Mystic beings, now appear!

SPIRITS' VOICES.

Mortal, ask not such a boon;
If we were to grant it, soon
You would all, like withered heath,
Blasted be by lightnings' breath
And would sink in instant death;
For whenever mortal eyes
Look on us that moment dies.

KING GREINE.

Mock me not with idle fears,
I have looked on your compeers,
Great and powerful as thou art,
And they could not shake my heart.

SPIRITS' VOICES.

Summoned by a milder spell,
We might then appear and tell

Thee of future things that lower,
But we're here in all our power,
Clad in panoply of light,
Which would blast all mortal sight!
Come, sweet spirits, let's away
Ere the opening hour of day.

KING GREINE.

Dread, mysterious beings, stay!
Leave us not without a sign
How this roaming Gadeline
May be driven from our shore
And their power quenched in gore.

SPIRITS' VOICES.

The four elements we bear—
Fire, water, earth, and air—
Mortal, call on any spright
That is hov'ring here to-night,
And you then may know the aid
Which we grant you ere we fade
Into beams of coming light,
And with them again unite!

II.

KING GREINE.

Come, mild spirit of the air,
We, thy magic children, dare
Ask what gift you can bestow,
That we may subdue the foe?

SPIRIT OF THE AIR.

I come at your call
From my airy hall,
In the clouds where I sport and play,
From Indian bowers,
Where I kiss the flowers,
And revel among them all day.
I sigh in the breeze
Of sweet Araby's trees,
Or dash through the foaming deep,
Where the thunder storm
Rears his misty form,
And the deadly typhoons sleep,
But ask me not ;—I may not say
Which of you will gain the day;
Yet I can some aid bestow
That will help you 'gainst the foe:
When upon the battle plain
Any of your men lie slain,
Ere their spirits gasp away
Touch them with a hazel spray,
And that moment they'll revive,
Strong and vigorously alive;
More I cannot do, nor tell,
Mortal, now farewell, farewell!

III.
KING CUILL.

Oh! thou of all the sprites that gleam
Through the ethereal space on high,

The brightest, purest, subtilest beam
That ever shone on mortal eye,

Come, spirit of fire, aid to-night
Thy children in to-morrow's fight

SPIRIT OF FIRE.

My throne is on the fires that glow
In the volcano's depths below;
I flash along the lightning's gleam,
Or glide upon the morning beam,
Just as my temper or my mood
Inclines to evil or to good,
And makes a paradise or waste
Where'er my rapid footsteps traced:
But we, the potent sprites of fire,
However much our own desire,
Cannot afford thee much relief
In thy anxiety and grief.
Though you have worshipped at our shrine
And offered to us rites divine,
Thy foemen too have worshipped there,
With purer faith and humbler prayer,
And never knelt to other powers,
But all their hearts and hopes were ours.
Yet what we can we will bestow
To help thee, 'gainst the coming foe;
A fierceness that no force can tame,
An ardour like a quenchless flame,

And courage that defeats renew,
These are the gifts we give to you.
Be prudent, use them wise and well,
Mortal we part—farewell! farewell!

IV.
KING CEAGHT.

Spirit of the waters, that sparklest with light,
Come in thy majesty, glory, and might,
  Come in thy bright array,
  And in the battle's fray,
  Sweep all our foes away,
Give us thy counsel and aid us to-night!

SPIRIT OF THE WATERS.

I come from my home in the deep blue sea,
  From sparry halls,
  And coral walls,
Where the dolphins shine and the sword-fish
 stray,
  From mountain streams,
  That flash in beams,
As they sport and laugh on their watery way;
  Where billows roar
  On the rocky shore,
And the water-spout madly flings his spray.
  Now listen well
  To what I tell:
  Watch well the plain
  Where lie the slain,

And ere from the heart
The last life-drop start,
Bathe well with dew
Brushed from the yew;
And if a spark of life remain
He will rise fierce and strong again!
Mortal, remember well this spell,
I can do no more, farewell, farewell!

CHORUS OF SPIRITS IN THE AIR.

We now go, the day is breaking
　Over mountain-top and plain,
Mortals will soon be awaking
　To begin life's toils again ;
While this orb is quickly gliding
　Every moment from our view
We, no more on earth abiding,
　Waft to thee our last adieu!
　　Adieu! Adieu!

ODE XVI.

THE LAST BATTLE.

I.

THE day rose bright o'er hill and dale,
Rich fragrance filled the morning gale,
And many an early flower of spring
Sent forth its dewy offering;
The hawthorn gave its rich perfume
Mingling with that of scented broom,

The cowslip from its dewy lid,
And star-like primroses half hid
In mossy nooks their incense sent
Up to the brightning firmament,
The deer roamed through the copse-wood glade
Or stalked along the grassy mead;
The hare limped over lonely spots
Where fern and wild forget-me-nots
And blue-bells under hazel bowers
Made one wild wilderness of flowers!
The morn was bright, the air was balm,
No sound to break the holy calm
That over Tailton reigned that day
Which ushered in the last of May.
But soon the clang of arms resounds
Along the silent, peaceful grounds,
And shouts of strife and yells of pain
Are wafted over all the plain,
And every swelling glade and glen
Resounds with tramp of armed men.

II.

The plains of Tailton, celebrated long
For classic games, festivity, and song, 80
Where kings and princes met in bright array,
To keep each year a national holiday;
To pitch the bar, to leap, to chase the roe,
To strike the targe with an unerring blow,

Or underneath the shade of some tall tree
To listen to soft strains of minstrelsy;
Ah, yes! those plains show now a different sight,
The bursting thunderstorm at dead of night
Can scarcely differ more from summer's ray
Than this lone place does now from yesterday.
As o'er the sky the dark clouds gather fast
In whirling shapes before the thunder blast,
So gather thick along the plains below
The Danaan forces and their daring foe,
Each squadron led by captains known to fame,
Triumphant victory their only aim;
Resolved to conquer or to bravely die
Before yon sun sinks in the western sky.
The Dananns fought for country, home, and sway,
Their sisters, wives, and little ones at play,
Their magic groves and consecrated dells,
The scenes of all their mystic charms and spells,
The lov'd ones that cling round them to the last,
All, all this day were staked upon a cast.
The fierce Milesians, with traditions long
Blazed forth in story and enshrined in song,
Which promised them in some mysterious way
That they should conquer on this fatal day,
Were nerved by hope and fired with deadly wrath
To sweep the treacherous Danaan from their path.
Wild thoughts of *Ith* wrapped on his bloody shroud[81]
Flashed through their souls, and called for vengeance loud

And deep and deadly as the fires that glow
And rage in Ætna's frearful depths below!
'Twas with such feelings both sides now engage,
To try the issue of war's deadly rage,
Determined never to survive the day,
Unless as victors, with unbounded sway.

III.

Ere modern science entered war's domain
    And smoothed down each hideous savage part,
When butchery triumphed o'er the fallen slain,
    And reckless courage mocked the rules of art,
The hostile force met upon the plain
In masses, and endeavoured, might and main,
To force each others' lines where all their strife
And power were centred, in contempt of life.

IV.

The Danaans were led on by their three kings,
    Sons of Cermada, Cuill, Ceaght and Greine;
Mac Greine led on the centre, both the wings
    Extended to the boundary of the plain
Each marshalled forth with battle cry, which rings
The diapason of the war, and brings
Heroic thoughts and courage to the soul
Which prudence could not, nor might skill control.

V.

The Danaan banners floated high in air,
  Their sacred raven, dappled with the blood
Of a young Danaan girl, bright and fair, [82]
  Rose in the centre, and around it stood
The magic guards:—'twas their peculiar care
To shield it round with mystic rite and prayer;
Their other colours on their folds display
The fiery dragon seizing on his prey.

VI.

Cuill and Ceaght command the left and right;
  One grasps the spear they brought from Odin's halls,
The other wields the sword supreme in fight
  Which their forefathers bore from Gorea's walls;
The magic cauldron flamed with lurid light,
As all the troops marched passed it in their might,
Glittering with charms that thick around them hung,
While their wild war-notes o'er the valley rung.

VII.

Milesian forces mustered fierce and strong,
  With Sunburst borne before the centre ranks, [83]
'Midst martial sounds from timbrel, harp, and gong
  Over the deep extended serried flanks
The serpent-banners, so renowned in song, [84]
Spread their broad folds, and as they move along
A hundred chiefs beneath their shadows stood,
Resolved to carve their way through fields of blood.

VIII.

The Druids, with Amhergin at their head,
  Were drawn up in the centre, robed in white ; ⁸⁵
The wings on both sides were by Heber led
  And Heremon, impatient for the fight.
A moment more, and who could count the dead
Or dying that from gaping wounds hath bled,
As o'er the field in mangled heaps they lay,
The fruits of victory, of war the prey!

IX.

Both armies charged in one unbroken mass,
  Compact and firm as a moving rock,
Until an opening through a bloody pass
  Was here and there effected by the shock
Of thousands trampling o'er the slippery grass,
Each trying who could in bold deeds surpass
His comrade's and advance his nation's claim,
To be emblazoned on the list of fame.

X.

Though cool at first, and cautious where to advance,
  And how to counteract each movement made
By the fierce foe, and leaving nought to chance,
  Yet, as the combat heightens, and they wade
High in their kindred's blood, the flashing lance
Alone decides the point ;—onward they prance
In reckless fury, heedless where they go,
So they can save a friend, or kill a foe.

XI.

Along the plain the scattered masses form,
   Like moonlight billows as casque, targe, spear,
And falchion flash in the soft light of morn,
   As back and forward in their wild career
They break, unite, and mingle in the storm
And whirl of battle : here and there a form
Gleams like a meteor over host of foes,
Till quenched, struck down at last in Death's repose,

XII.

Some straggle up and down the ensanguined plain,
   Uphold the fight, in groups of two or three,
And some in single combat still maintain
   Their ancient prowess, and seek victory
In deeds of daring, shedding blood like rain,
Till but a few fierce spirits yet remain,
Like some few stars that shine in morning's ray,
And yield not even to the beams of day.

XIII.

Still three large groups of warriors kept the field,
   And fought in compact masses, far apart;
Now the Danaans, now the Milesians yield
   As falchions, blade, or javelin pierce the heart.
And many a headless trunk, and broken shield,
And severed arm, that could no longer wield
The ponderous axe, lay scattered far and wide,
And dead and dying foes lay side by side.

XIV.

Amhergin and Mac Greine met in the fight—
 They sought to meet each other all the day ;—
And now the carnage thickens left and right
 As each draw nearer in the bloody fray.
The Gadel prince wielded with all his might
An axe, whose sweep forever quenched the light
Of many a chief who, till the time he fell,
Was deemed by all to be invincible.

XV.

The Danaan prince fought with the magic spear,
 And as he waved it o'er him to-and-fro
Blue flickering light around him did appear
 In coruscations of the brightest glow,
Which caused the bravest heart, as they drew near
To pause and falter in their wild career;
He bore down all before him like a flood,
Till face to face the rival leaders stood.

XVI.

The long-sought hour for vengeance came at last.
 Short was the conflict, for too well they knew
Fame, freedom, life itself were on the cast,
 Nor paused, nor wavered, but with instinct true
To the traditions of their glorious past,
Rushed to the conflict 'midst blows fierce and fast,
Until the axe gleamed for a moment o'er
The Danaan prince, and closed his life in gore,

XVII.

Then as Amhergin swept along the plain,
  He saw the Druids of the Danaan force
Move slowly up and down among the slain;
  And as they passed along, each mangled corse
Rose fierce and furious to begin again
The deadly conflict, and he felt how vain
Was all their valour, since these could restore
Life to the slain to charge their foes once more.

XVIII.

He felt there was no antidote in store,
  No counter charm for practices like those,
Save to stamp out the occult art in gore,
  And quench the light of magic with their foes.
He therefore charged into their midst before
They were aware of his intent, and bore
Down all before him like the simoom's blast,
Quenching the light of life where'er he passed

XIX.

'Twas not till then the Danaan valour fled ;
  They shrunk nor quailed not all the livelong day,
Until they saw one of their princes dead,
  And all his magic powers fade away.
When they beheld the enchanted guards, who led
The charge so often from their gory bed,
Silent and prostrate on the cold grass lie,
They knew their doom—to fight awhile and die !

XX.

And they did fight, and boldly kept the field,
   Retreating slowly on before the foe,
Beaten and broken, still they would not yield,
   But often stopped and turned to deal a blow
With all the energy despair could wield,
And with the act died on the bloody shield;
Yet, all the valour of the fierce Mac Ceaght
Could not avail them or prevent retreat.

XXI.

As in a surging sea with billows high
   Two boats are tossed about, sometimes quite near,
Then widely parted, and again come nigh,
   And then are dashed together, such appear
Mac Cuill and Heber, each resolved to die,—
They fought as if they both could fate defy,
And warriors stood round in fierce delight
And silent wonder as they viewed the fight.

XXII.

The parried thrust, the well-aimed, vigorous blow,
   The practised feint, the sudden furious dash,
These all were tried, and blood began to flow,
   When Heber, maddened by a gaping gash,
Sprang like a tiger on his stubborn foe;
Then flashed the sabre, and the deadly blow
Cut down Mac Cuill: ere he reached the ground
His soul flew shrieking through the quivering wound.

XXIII.

Just like the full-orbed moon when mists arise,
   And darkened clouds obscure its magic light,
When storms career along the glowing skies,
   Which change the aspect of advancing night,
So fell the gloom on Danaan hope that tries
In vain to cope with adverse destinies;
Mac Ceaght of all the royal house alone
Still dauntlessly contends for life and throne.

XXIV.

But tries in vain, the panic is complete,
   The rout is general, all are borne along;
Still the king wrestles bravely against fate,
   And stems the tide of the bewildered throng.
But valour fails to nerve or elevate
The flying squadrons to their former state,
And courage only now protracts the strife
And causes greater sacrifice of life.

XXV.

At length beside a little hill they stand,
   Determined there to end the unequal strife,
Mac Ceaght, still dauntless, towering, and grand,
   Resolved to close the scene with his own life.
Collecting all the force he could command,
He turned, with this devoted little band,
And there encountered Heremon face to face
And died the last, the bravest of his race.

XXVI.

The leaders met, it was the first and last
    Time they should meet on earth;—the life of one,
Perhaps of both, they knew was drawing fast
    To death's dark close, and fate was hastening fast,
The present to be shortly of the past;
For quick and furious as the thunder-blast
They assail each other with tremendous blows,
And solid armour's rent, and life-blood flows.

XXVII.

They close at last: the weapons thrown away,
    As useless as a slender willow wand;
And though the battle raged so fierce all day,
    They unexhausted combat hand-to-hand,
And Laocoon-like seizing upon the prey,
Then twine around each other, and essay
By strength and prowess at one blow to sever
The rival claims of victory forever!

XXVIII.

They separate, but only to renew
    The fearful struggle! Each a weapon caught:
Mac Ceaght a shining falchion fiercely drew,
    Mac Heremon whirled the spear with which he fought
With giant force and aim so fixed and true
That, like an arrow's shaft, it quickly flew,
And entering deep into the Danaan's brain,
He fell the last, the greatest of the slain.

XXIX.

The war was over when King Mac Ceaght fell
  And shouts of triumph filled the battle field
Despite of Danaan valour, charm, and spell,
  They were obliged by fate at last to yield,
Though even defeat could not that spirit quell;
And they have left for other times to tell
How fiercely they maintained till their last breath
Their independence till it closed in death!

Ode XVII.

The conclusion.

My task is done, my song is o'er,
My clearsach shall be heard no more,
Its strings are broken and unstrung,
Its last expiring note is sung,
And, Phœnix-like, will sink to rest
With music flowing from its breast;
Though coldness, and neglect, and time
Have robbed it of its sweetest chime,
I could not bear to tear away
Its strings without a closing lay
To those dim records of the past,
That in despite of time still last,
And shine along through Erin's page,
Mellowed and mystified by age,

Like those old towers, which they say,
Lie 'neath the billows of Lough Neagh,
But having closed this votive strain,
I ne'er shall wake its strains again,
And only linger on to say
To those who listened to my lay,
Accept those thanks my feelings tell
Are found within that word farewell!

NOTES.

NOTES.

1 Page 10.—The Chinese-rose is a delicate species of the blush-rose, whose tints have been, not inappropriately, compared by the eastern poets to the first bright blushes of daybreak. It was first brought to this country by Lord Macartney, Ambassador to the Court of China, in 1793. He also brought another rose from China at the same time, which is still called by his name, the Macartney Rose. (See Anderson's "China.")

2 Page 12.—" The sides of the mountains become larger, grander, and more barren as we advance. By little and little the scanty vegetation fades and dies, even the mosses disappear, and the rocks which at first were quite white, are tinged with a red and white burning hue. In the middle of this plain there is a dry and parched basin, enclosed on all sides by hills scattered over with a yellow-coloured pebble. On one side are ruined buildings stunted cypresses, and bushes of the aloe and the prickly pear, on the other a number of heavy square massive buildings. This spot is Jerusalem." (Cabinet Library.)

3 Page 15.—" Hesperides of old " is supposed to have been situated in the north-west of Africa, at the feet of the Atlas Mountains.

4 Page 15.—Many are of opinion that here was the birth-place of Homer, and it is affirmed that part of the Iliad was written here before he went to Greece.

Page 15.—The " Sacred Mount," Mount Parnassus.

⁶ Page 16.—Though the remains of ancient buildings have been discovered in and about Mexico, and some temples of great architectural beauty were in a high state of preservation, and covered all over with silver when the Spaniards first invaded that part of the world; yet, as they do not often occur in that vast continent, I have taken the liberty used in the above lines.

⁷ Page 16.—"Far in the immense woods we met with several lakes of great beauty and extent but without a name." (Humboldt.)

⁸ Page 17.—"The sun, looking majestically through the descending spray, was encircled by a radiant halo, while fragments of rainbows floated on every side, and momentarily vanished, only to give place to a succession of others more brilliant." (Howison.)

⁹ Page 17.—For many interesting particulars of the Arctic Regions, see voyages of Captains Parry and Ross.

¹⁰ Page 17.—"The Land of Lakes"—the Canadas.

¹¹ Page 18.—"Earthquakes were unknown in Quito until a comparatively late period; but since they have made their appearance they have not only altered the natural appearance of the country, but the climate has become colder and more inclement." (Murphy's and Thomson's Geography.)

¹² Page 18.—Buenos Ayres is the native region of the Condar.

¹³ Page 19.—See Sir Walter Raleigh's account of the vast regions of Brazil, &c.

¹⁴ Page 19.—The inhabitants of Patagonia are said to be generally from seven to eight feet high. For a lengthened description of Patagonia and its inhabitants, see "Life among the Giants."

¹⁵ Page 19.—For a description of the Isles of the Pacific, and an account of the manners and customs of the people, see Cook's "Voyages to the Pacific," and Lord Byron's poem of the island.'

Page 21.—The Acropolis was a citadel and not a place of

religious worship; but near it are the ruins of the temples of Minerva and the Sun. Probably it is in some measure excusable in an Irishman to suppose *every ruin* to be a *place of worship*.

17 Page 22.—The author of "Letters from the Mediterranean" says that the waters of the Archipelago and the Levant are sometimes of a purple and orange colour, and that they often shine in the evenings with phosphoric light. Subsequent scientific inquiry has discovered that this is owing to the presence of myriads of animalcules with which the waters are impregnated.

18 Page 25.—Mount Hecla has been an extinct volcano these many years, while the wonderful phenomenon, the Geysers, continue in active operation. (See Murphy's Large Geography.)

19 Page 26.—For a description of a gathering of the Highland clans and their preparation for warfare, see the "Lady of the Lake," Mac Pherson's "Antiquities," and Scott's "Tales of a Grandfather."

20 Page 27.—England's career through the world has been marked with ruin and slavery, carried on under the specious pretext of civilisation and improvement. Any unprejudiced reader of her history cannot possibly come to any other conclusion.

21 Page 31.—We have the authority of several Irish historians for affirming, that in the days of our country's chivalry and glory her warriors and native princes, after securing liberty at home, frequently carried the fame of their arms in the same sacred cause even to the foot of the Alps. (See Keating's, Mac Geoghegan's, and Mac Dermott's Histories of Ireland.)

22 Page 32.—For an account of the "veto," which had for its manifest object the separation of the interests of the clergy from the people, see the brilliant account of it in the "Ecclesiastical History of Ireland," by the Rev. M. J. Brenan, O.S.F.

Ireland at that time presented a scene worthy of the purest days of the Greek and Roman republics—an oppressed people refusing honour and liberty on the condition of making any compromise with the discipline of their ancient faith—a beloved priesthood refusing British gold, though suffering all the privations of that poor but faithful people.

23 Page 32.—How beautiful and sublime are all the ceremonies of the Catholic Church! Ever solicitous for the welfare of all her children, she never forgets in her devotions the absent nor the dead.

24 Page 33.—The ancient Romans had no higher idea of grandeur or magnificence than the triumphal entry of their Generals, Consuls, and Dictators after a victorious battle. (Goldsmith.)

25 Page 34.—The Emperors Julius and Augustus Cæsar were deified even in their lifetime by their impious courtiers. Caligula built temples to his sister, Drusilla, and commanded himself to be adored as a god (See Brown's Roman History, and the History of the Roman Empresses.)

26 Page 35.—Upon the demise of his father, Constantius Cloves, who died in Great Britain, Constantine was there proclaimed emperor in 306. His first care was, though not yet a Christian, to prohibit all persecution in the western provinces, which were under his dominion. (History of the Church, by Seig. Pastorini.)

27 Page 37.—The grand portal of St. Peter is opened only once a year—on Easter Sunday—to admit the gorgeous procession of cardinals, bishops, and high dignataries of the Church to the high altar to be present at the solemn pontifical High Mass, which on such occasions is always celebrated by His Holiness in person. (See Rev. Dr. Gahan's, or Rev. Dr. Reeve's History of the Church.)

28 Page 37.—This was written before the spoliation of the Church took place by Victor Emmanuel.

29 Page 37.—There is such uniformity in all the ceremonies of the Catholic Church, that no matter how far the Catholic

travels, or how widely different the country may be in customs, manners, laws, and language from his own, yet in assisting at any of the public ceremonies he always feels at home.

30 Page 38.—The word "Sabbath," according to Josephus, is derived from the Assyrian-Chaldean language, and literally means day of rest.

31 Page 39.—"The tears of repentance are sweeter and more agreeable, without any comparison, than all the pleasures of the theatre." (St. Augustine.)

32 Page 49.—"In less than two years after the first inquisition, Henry VIII. became possessed of all the monastic revenues. . . . The whole of the suppressed monasteries amounted to 645, of which 28 had abbots, who enjoyed a seat in parliament. 90 colleges were demolished in several counties; 2,375 chantries and free chapels, and 110 hospitals. The whole revenues of these establishments amounted to £161,000, which was about the twentieth part of the national income of that day." (Hume's "History of England.")

33 Page 51.—The *Times'* Commissioner sent over to Ireland to report on the agricultural prospects and general condition of the country.

34 Page 54.—This is something after the plan of giving a severe and almost incurable wound, and then, sending a quack-doctor to *probe* it, who, after torturing the patient in every possible way, apparently for his own amusement, at length very gravely pronounces it incurable.

35 Page 58.—The broad, brilliant moon of September is generally called the "Harvest Moon," as it gives welcome light to the farmer and cottier in mountain districts, where crops are later, to gather in the harvest after daylight at that busy season of the year.

36 Page 62.—An old inhabitant of Wexford told me, many years ago, that he remembered the last bell which was sent from our shores to England. I believe it was the bell of St. Patrick's,

one of the parochial churches of the town; and it is somewhat remarkable, that, though it was in the summer season, and the weather uncommonly fine, the vessel that bore it away had scarcely put to sea when a violent storm arose and she sank into the deep waters near the Wexford coast.

37 Page 63.—It is, or rather was the belief of the peasantry in many parts of Ireland, that all the treasure buried in the country is under enchantment. There is scarcely an old church or castle that has not been the scene of many a midnight excavation; and it is the general opinion that the golden treasure is guarded by some spirit or demon, or by the soul of the deceased person who buried it.

38 Page 65.—The first battle fought between the English and Irish was in the county Wexford, not far from the place where the English landed. It has been appropriately called Battlestown.

39 Page 66.—" Wexford is slow—but Wexford is sure." (Words taken from a speech of O'Connell.)

40 Page 69.—The county Wexford, in particular, Dr. M'Nevin supposed to have supplied so many as 40,000 to the Insurrection of 1798; great numbers, after its extinction, volunteered into the British force, preparing to expel the French from Egypt. Numbers also who were sentenced to transportation preferred joining the expedition. . . . The subsequent distinguished bravery of the "Men of Wexford" is briefly adverted to by Hay in his history of the Wexford Insurrection. The insurgents, according to the commentator of "Tone's Life," were also considerably influenced to join the British expedition to Egypt, by a wish to revenge on the French the apparently faithless desertion of Ireland by the *Republic*. (See the "Green Book.")

41 Page 85.—These lines were written during the time of O'Connell's magnificent monster meetings, when the heart of

reland was stirred in a manner never felt before or since in any age or country.

⁴² Page 86.—RED HUGH O'DONNELL died at Simancas, in Spain, on the 10th of September, 1602. He was buried, by order of the king with royal honours, as befitting a prince of Kinnel-Conal; and the Chapter of the Cathedral of St. Francis, in the stately city of Valladolid, holds the bones of as noble a chief and as stout a warrior as ever bore the wand of a chieftain, or led a clan to battle. (Mitchel's " Life of Hugh O'Donnell.")

⁴³ Page 86.—SARSFIELD was slain on the 29th of July, 1693, at *Landen*, while heading his countrymen in the van of victory, King William flying. As he lay on the field, unhelmed and dying, he put his hand to his breast. When he took it away it was full of his best blood. Looking at it sadly, with an eye in which victory shone a moment before, he said, faintly, " Oh, that this was for Ireland!" (Davis.)

⁴⁴ Page 86.—LORD EDWARD FITZGERALD died in one of the cells of Newgate, from the effects of a wound which he received in the neck when gallantly struggling with his captors. (See Moore's "Life of Lord Edward Fitzgerald.")

⁴ Page 89.—"Cormac Ulla" and "Mac Ossian" were the *noms de plume* of other song-writers of the *Wexford Independent*.

⁴⁶ Page 90.—The "Red Coats"—the name given by the peasantry of the county Wexford to the soldiers. I have often heard my poor countrywomen, who were witnesses of the brutal atrocities of the soldiers of '98, declare that they could never look upon a man with a *red coat* without feelings of horror.

⁴⁷ Page 94.—The places mentioned were the scenes of the meetings of several Bardic Sessions held, or rather supposed to be held, by the poetical contributors of the *Wexford Independent*.

⁴⁸ Page 108.—The young Geraldine, Silken Thomas.

⁴⁹ Page 109.—These stanzas were written at the time of O'Connell's incarceration in Richmond Prison.

50 Page 117.—From the top of Croghan Mountain an extensive view can be had of several parts of the county Wexford; the places mentioned in the text can be distinctly seen from it on a clear day.

51 Page 118.—" CORMAC ULLA," one of the song-writers of the *Wexford Independent*. James Mac Grady, who adopted the above, was one of the purest patriots and the most guileless beings in existence. Gifted with an extraordinary power of mind and memory, and possessing an exuberant fancy and cultivated intellect, he was apparently unconscious of these rich gifts, and to the knowledge and judgment of the philosopher he added the simplicity and innocence of a little child. Mac Grady was editor of the *Wexford Independent* for several years, and was the promoter of the Bardic Sessions.

52 Page 119.*—It is the opinion of some that the stone over the " Croppies' Grave," on the Hill of Tara, is the celebrated *Lia Fail*, or Stone of Destiny, upon which the Milesian kings of Ireland were crowned for several centuries. Others, however, with a better reason, assert that the real Stone of Destiny is at present under the Coronation Chair in Westminster.

53 Page 127.—This was written when O'Connell was playing with *Federalism*.

54 Page 131.—The old whitethorn-tree has been, time out of mind, dedicated to the Irish fairy; and, indeed, they could not bestow on it a sweeter offering.

55 Page 144.—" That rocky glen " is a very romantic spot, near Wexford, called Carrig. It was often the scene of my youthful rambles.

56 Page 194.—In the notes to "Lalla Rookh," Moore says it is supposed by the Eastern poets that the amber found in such quantities on the shores of the Sea of Oman is formed by the tears of birds.

---

* The several persons alluded to in the text were persons who contributed to the *Independent* under these names.

NOTES.   333

57 Page 217.—" Donald of Shielmaliere " was the signature used by Martin M'Donald Doyle in his poetical contributions to the *Wexford Independent*. He was principally instrumental in evoking the native talent of Wexford, and inaugurating the " Songs of the *Independent*," which rivalled the contemporary Press of Ireland, and got a wide circulation in native and American journals. He was a native of Bannow, county Wexford, and from an early age evinced great poetical ability. That erudite and polished scholar, Thomas Boyse, introduced young Doyle to the poet Moore when he visited Bannow, and under their auspices he published a volume of poems, which were alike worthy of the author and of such distinguished patronage.

58 Page 217.—The *Wexford Independent*.

59 Page 218.—These were the names of the places where the song-writers of the *Wexford Independent* were supposed to hold their Bardic Sessions.

60 Page 219.—" Glenalvon " was the signature used by another of the song-writers of the *Wexford Independent*. Like " Rosaloo," and " Donald of Shielmaliere," he was a native of Wexford. His name was Nicholas Corish, and for three or four years he contributed many beautiful pieces of poetry to the " Songs."

61 Page 255.—Ireland was called, in the time of the Druids, the " Sacred Isle," from being the chief seat of their religion and it was afterwards called the " Island of Saints " in the earlier ages of Christianity, from the great number of saints and sages it produced and sent out to preach the Gospel to distant heathen nations. (See O'Halloran's " Ireland.")

62 Page 256.—" Saint Ibar's Isle " is a small island, called *Beg-Erin* (Little Ireland), to the north of Wexford Harbour. This secluded and neglected spot is celebrated by all the Irish historians. Here St. IBAR, or IBBERIUS, founded a college and monastery prior to the arrival of St. Patrick, where he taught the arts and sciences, as well as the sublime mysteries of religion gratuitously to thousands of distinguished natives as well as foreigners, who resorted thither from all parts of Europe. It was the first and most famous seat of Christian literature at that time in the world, and existed prior to Clonmacnoise, Jerpont, Clonard, and the other celebrated Irish colleges, which subsequently rose to such eminence. Scarcely a trace of those ruins remain at the present day. The walls of a very small building, probably a chapel, rise a few feet above the surface; the masonry is very rude and irregular, of what is called *cyclopean*, which proves its great antiquity. This is all that at present remain of the far-famed schools of St. Ibar. (See Rev. M. J. Brenan's "Ecclesiastical History of Ireland.")

63 Page 258.—Not only the church property in lands and tenements, but the sacred edifices themselves, were torn from the owners and bestowed on the despoilers.

64 Page 267.—"I've wandered far to Croghan's height." One of the Wicklow mountains, and the scene of one of the Bardic Sessions of the song-writers of the *Wexford Independent*.

65 Page 267.—"They met in that black year of night." The year of famine in Ireland, 1847.

66 Page 268.—"And where are they, the faithful band." The song-writers of the *Wexford Independent*.

67 Page 269.—"He stood upon his lonely hill,
       And leaned upon the Dead Man's Chair."
The "Dead Man's Chair" is the highest point on Croghan Mountain—another scene of the Bardic Session.

68 Page 269.—"'Tis he, the last old *Senachie!*" A bard, historian, and poet of the olden time. Under the Milesian Government these were a privileged class, and ranked in the social scale next after the royal family. They were allowed to wear six colours in their plaids. The royal family and their immediate descendants alone wore seven colours.

69 Page 274.—"At that bright spot where their young Day-

God blazed." The chief object of adoration with the Milesians was the sun.

70 Page 277.—"To where they fancied lay old Inbher Slainge." The ancient name of Wexford, at the mouth of the Slaney. The old name of this river was *Slainge*.

71 Page 279.—"Bright as in ZOROASTER'S days!" The Magi were a religious sect of the ancient Eastern nations of the world, of which Persia was the principal. The Persians and Chaldeans cultivated astronomy at a very early age, and were the first to worship the sun as the visible impersonation of the Divinity. The Wise Men of the East, who were the first Gentile worshippers of the Infant Saviour, are supposed to have been of this sect. Zoroaster was the founder, and is the first on record who adored *fire* and the *sun*. (See Rollin's "Ancient History.")

72 Page 279.—"Our destined place of final rest." Prince Amhergin, who was also high priest, or Arch-Druid, reminded them of the ancient prophecy of CAICER, the Arch-Druid of their nation. He informed them that Ireland, which was unknown in the time of CAICER, was the country destined for their final home. (See Mac Dermott's "History of Ireland.")

73 Page 280.—THE STORM. "The Milesian fleet first attempted to land upon the south-eastern coast of Leinster at a place called Inbher Slainge, now known as the Harbour of Wexford. The De Danaans, alarmed at the number of the ships, immediately flocked to the sea shore, and by the power of their enchantments and diabolical arts they cast such a cloud over the whole island that the Milesians were confounded, and thought they saw nothing but the resemblance of a hog." (Keating.)

74 Page 282.—"Until they came to Inbher Colpa's Bay." "When the Milesian ships were parted by the storm, the portion commanded by Heremon landed at Inbher-Colpa (Drogheda), so called from Colpa, the swordsman, one of the Milesian princes who perished there." (Mac Geoghegan.)

⁷⁵ Page 282.—"but most
Of all the rest made Inbher Secine's shore."
"Heber and Amhergin, who commanded the other portion of the squadron, landed at Inbher Secine, now called Bantry Bay." (Mac Geoghegan.)

⁷⁶ Page 283.—"Jacob's consecrated stone." Some Irish writers assert that the celebrated *Lia Fail*, or Stone of Destiny, was the identical stone which the patriarch Jacob put under his head when he had the vision of angels; and that Moses gave it to an ancestor of Milesius on the banks of the Red Sea, in acknowledgment for assistance rendered to the Israelites in their flight from Egypt. This stone had the singular property of emitting sounds resembling thunder when any of the true Milesians were crowned on it. The same is related of the statue of Memnon, in the Thebaid, which uttered an articulate sound when it received the first rays of the rising sun. Herodotus says he heard this sound himself from the Sphinx, when he visited the great Pyramid. The *Lia Fail* is now under the Coronation Chair in Westminster Abbey.

⁷⁷ Page 284.—"O'er the broad valleys of high Slieve-na-Mis." "The fleet of the sons of Milesius came to Ireland at the end of the year of the world 3500, to take it from the Tuatha Da Danaans, and fought the first battle at Sliahb Mis with them on the third day after landing." ("Annals of the Four Masters.")

⁷⁸ Page 289.—"She faintly faltered 'Victory,' and dies." "In this battle fell Scota, the daughter of Pharaoh, King of Egypt, and wife of Milesius. She was buried the next day with great pomp and magnificence in a valley called to this day '*Glen Scota.*'" (Keating.)

⁷⁹ Page 303.—"By this thrice enchanted spear." "The De Danaans brought a magic spear, a magic sword, and a magic cauldron with them from Scandinavia to Ireland." (Keating.)

⁸⁰ Page 309.—"The plains of Tailton, celebrated long."
For classic games, festivity, and song."

"Luigha, the long-handed, was the institutor of the famous games at Tailton. They were celebrated in honour of Tailte, queen of the last monarch of the Belgæ. After their defeat she was married to a Danaan chief, and was entrusted with the education of the young Prince Luigha, who in gratitude for the care and tenderness experienced from her, established this Assembly to commemorate her name. The games were celebrated every year in the first of autumn for thirty days." (Mac Dermott.)

Tailton is a plain situate in the county Meath. The tomb of Queen Tailte was visible here until three or four hundred years ago. The place is now occupied by the little village of Tellton, in Meath.

81 Page 310.—"Wild thoughts of *Ith* wrapped in his bloody shroud." Ith was the first Milesian who landed in Ireland. He was received in the most friendly manner by the Danaan princes; but on his return to his ship was set upon and most treacherously slain by the Danaans." (Keating.)

82 Page 312.—The sacred raven dappled with the blood "of a young Danaan girl bright and fair." The raven was worshipped by the Danaans, and its figure imprinted on their chief banners. A young girl was frequently sacrificed, and her blood sprinkled on their banners before going to battle.

83 Page 312.—"The Sunburst borne before the centre ranks." The Sunburst was the chief standard of the Milesians. It was magnificently decorated with gems and gold, and represented the sun rising through the golden clouds of the East. It was almost worshipped by the Milesians, and carried with them in all their wanderings.

84 Page 312.—"The serpent banners, so renowned in song." When Moses was on the banks of the Red Sea leading the Israelites out of Egypt, he was met by Niul, the great master of the Milesians, who reigned as a sovereign and independent prince at *Capacriunt*, near the place where Moses was encamped. Niul, alarmed at such a vast number of persons encamped in his

vicinity, inquired of Moses who they were and the cause of their arrival. Aaron gave him a brief account of the Hebrew nation, and the bondage to which they had been subjected by the Egyptians. Niul, affected by the relation, proffered him assistance, and offered to supply him with corn and such necessaries as the country produced. It happened on the same night that the young prince Gadel was bitten by a serpent. The venom quickly diffused itself through his veins, so that he was soon reduced to the last extremity. Niul, alarmed at this fatal accident, and knowing the miraculous powers of Moses, carried the expiring prince to the camp of the Israelites, and entreated Moses that he would heal his son. Moses complied with the anxious request of the afflicted parent, and laying a rod which he held in his hand on the wound, the young prince immediately recovered. The place of the wound remained marked with a green spot, from which some etymologists derive the additional name *Glas* (green), which he took, and hence derive one of the names by which his posterity was known, that of *Gadelians*, the descendants of *Gadel-gase* i. e. *Gadel of the green mark*. Moses, having performed the miraculous cure, prophesied that wherever the young prince or his posterity should inhabit would be free from all venomous creatures. Hence on all their banners, except the *Sunburst*, the form of a green snake was emblazoned.

85 Page 313.—The Druids, were drawn up in the centre, robed in white, with, Amhergin at their head. *White* was the official dress of the Druids.

LIST OF SUBSCRIBERS.

A.

ARCHER, Miss M., Wexford.
Armstrong, Miss Alice, William-street, Wexford.
Armstrong, John, Esq., Compton House, Church-street, Liverpool.

B.

Barry, John, M.P.
Byrne, Garrett M., M. P., Wicklow.
Browne, Rev. James, P.P., Piercestown.
Brady, Mr. Thomas, Duncormack
Boggin, John, Esq., Tinnacurra, Clearistown.
Breen, P. J., Esq., Professor of Music.
Bent, Master Thomas, Hill-street, Wexford.
Barry, Richard, Esq., Wexford.
Ball, Mr. Alexander, Morick-street, ,,
Boggan, Rev. J., C.C., Ballymitty.
Byrne, Mr. John, Blackwater.
Busher, Very Rev. Thomas, P.P., Newtownbarry.
Barry, Rev. Sylvester, Professor, All Hallows College, Dublin.
Barry, Miss Bridget, Bannow.
Barry, William, Esq., Rowe-street, Cork.
Breen, J. P., Esq., New-street, Wexford.
Brennan, Miss Anne.
Barry, B., Esq., Sea-view, Bannow.
Byrne, Mr. John, Duncormack.
Bolger, Mr. James, Lambert-place, Wexford.
Bolger, Mr. Patrick, Rathnure.
Buckley, John, Esq., South Main-street, Wexford.
Brien, Denis, Esq., ,, ,,
Breen, Mr. Richard L., Quay, ,,

LIST OF SUBSCRIBERS

Brennan, Miss M., Ballintra, Co. Donegal.
Bonner, Mr. John,   ,,   ,,
Browne, Mrs., Fardystown.
Bolger, E., Esq., St. Aidan's Academy, Enniscorthy.
Byrne, Philip, Esq., Wexford.
Bell, James, Esq., Upper Hope-place, Liverpool.
Barry, John E., Esq., Faythe House, Wexford.
Bourke, Patrick, Esq., Wexford.
Byrne, Mr. Patrick, Bullring.
Brady, Mr. Stephen, Galbally.
Byrne, Mr. Benjamin, Killashee.
Barron, Mr. John, Barntown.
Brien, Peter, Esq., Coolamain.
Brennan, B., Esq., Taghmon.
Breslan, P. J., Esq., architect, Wexford.
Butler, Thomas, R.I.C., Castlebridge.
Barton, Miss Mary,   ,,

C.

Cousins, Patrick, Esq., North Main-street, Wexford.
Cowman, Luke, Esq.,   ,,   ,,
Clarke, C., Esq., Port Louis, Mauritius.
Casey, P. M., Esq., Enniscorthy.
Clarke, Miss Mary, Ballyboggan.
Christian Brothers, Wexford.
Cloke, Patrick, Esq., New York (10 copies).
Codd, Nicholas, Esq., Homestown.
Cardiff, Doctor, Carrigbyrne.
Cullen, Nicholas T., Esq., Cornmarket, Wexford.
Cleary, Mr. John, Queen's County.
Crean, Robert, J., Physician and Surgeon.
Coughlan, William, J.P., Summerville.
Connell, Mrs. M., Bethiville.
Caulfield, W. A., J.P., Wexford.
Cleary, Mr. Michael, Coolcots.
Connick, William, Esq., Main-street, Wexford.
Crosby, Denis, Esq., Grague, Bannow.
Cloney, Rev. Thomas, P.P., Tagoot.
Conway, Mr. John, Loughlinstown.
Coughlan, Miss Anne, Summerville.
Codd, Thomas, Esq., Ringbawn.
Colfer, Mr. Joseph, Kilmore.
Cleary, Henry W., Esq., Glenreamy, Oulart, Gorey.

LIST OF SUBSCRIBERS.   3

Corcoran, Mr. William, Selskar.
Cavanagh, Rev. Matthew E., C.C., Barntown.
Conway, A., Clk., A.B., Holly Fort, Gorey"(2 copies).
Codd, Miss Mary Jane, Taghmon.
Cahill, Rev. Thomas, P.P., Ballymore.
Colathan, Mr. Thomas, Wexford.
Cloney, Rev. Sylvester, P.P., Kilrush, Clohamon.
Crosby, Thomas, Esq., Carrig Hill.
Codd, Mark, Esq., Garse.
Corish, Rev. John, C.C., Monageer.
Corish, Rev. P. A., O. S. F., Wexford.
Corish, Rev. John, C.C., Newtownbarry.
Corish, James, Esq., Harveystown.
Callaghan, Patrick H. C., R.I.C., George's-street, Wexford.
Cavanagh, Denis, Esq., Maynooth.
Cullen, A. M., Bay, Bannow.
Cullen, Mrs. K., Duncormack.
Coughlan, Miss Margaret, Duncormack.
Cullen, Walter, Esq.,   ,,
Crean, Rev. M. E., St. Peter's College, Wexford.
Collier, W. M., Esq., H.M.I.R., Dell-road, Campbelltown.
Coleman, Michael, Esq., Collector Inland Revenue, Kilkenny.
Cradock, J., Esq.,   ,,   ,,   Waterford.
Codd, Nicholas, Esq., South Main-street, Wexford.
Coughlan, Miss Mary, Connaught-square, Hyde Park, London.
   (4 copies).
Catholic Young Men's Society, Wexford.
Cahill, Mr. P., Cushinstown.
Carr, Miss Annie, New-street, Wexford.
Carr, Matthew, Esq.,   ,,

D.

Daunt, W. J. O'Neill, Esq., Kilcascan.
Doyle, Stephen, T. C., John-street, Wexford.
Doyle, Mr. Stephen, Cornmarket,   ,,
Devereux, Laurence, Esq., South Main-street, Wexford
Devereux, William, B., Esq., Distillery House,   ,,
Donohoe, Mr. John, South Main-street,   ,,
Doyle, Rev. John, St. Peter's College,   ,,
Doran, Very Rev. Myles, P.P., Castlebridge.
Doyle, Very Rev. Edward, P.P., Ballymurn.
Dake, Stephen, Esq., Bannow.
Devereux, Mr. Patrick, Piercestown.

LIST OF SUBSCRIBERS.

Doyle, Patrick, Esq., Redmond-place, Wexford.
Devereux, Richard J., Esq., Summer-hill, ,,
Devereux, Mrs. Richard J., ,, ,,
Dixon, George, Esq., Main-street, ,,
Devereux, James P., Esq., Rocklands.
Doyle, Rev. John, C.C., Ferns.
Doyle, Myles, Esq., Wexford.
Devereux, William J., ,,
Dunne, Mr. John, Killahard.
Dingwall, Thomas J., Queenstown, Cork.

E

Eakins, Walter, Esq., Richmond-terrace, Wexford
English, Nicholas T., Esq., ,,
Ennis, A. M., Esq., Rowe-street ,,
English, Mrs. Catherine, School-street, ,,
Ennis, Rev. B. I., Anne-street, ,,
Eyre, John, Esq., White's Hotel, ,,

F

Foley, Very Rev. Denis, P.P., Glynn.
Fortune, Thomas J., Esq., Brown's Castle, Wexford.
Fortune, William, Esq., ,,
Finn, Michael, Esq., ,,
Feur, James, Esq., ,,
Ffrench, Peter, Esq., Harpoonstown.
Fortune, Very Rev. Doctor, All Hallows College, Dublin.
Fortune, Richard, Esq., H. C., Quay, Wexford.
Fenelon, James, Esq., Moneyhore.
Faris, David, Esq., Wexford.
Furlong, John, Esq., Scoby.
Farrell, James, Esq., Wexford.
French, William, Esq., New-street, Wexford.
Furlong, Rev. J. W., P.P., Cushinstown.
Franklin, Mr. John, Taghmon.
Fardy, Peter, Esq., South Main-street, Wexford.
Furlong, Patrick, Esq., Anne-street, ,,
Fortune, Ambrose R., T.C. and H.C., ,,
Fardy, William J., Esq., Port Louis, Mauritius.
FitzSimon, John, Esq., North Main-street, Wexford.
Furlong, Richard, J., Esq., Broad-street, Charleston, South Carolina.
Furlong, Matthew J., Esq., South Main-street, Wexford.

LIST OF SUBSCRIBERS.

G

Greene, John, J.P., Mount Anna, Wexford.
Gethings, John, Esq.,   ,,
Grey, John, Esq., Dublin.
Gifford, J. N., Esq., Wexford.
Goodall, Abraham, Esq., Roslare Fort, Wexford.
Gafney, W, J., Esq., Postmaster, Wexford.
Graham, John, Esq., Tullymorneen, Co. Donegal.
Gallagher, Rev. F., C.C., Ballintra,   ,,

H.

Holbrook, Patrick, Esq., Wexford.
Hayes, William James, Esq.,   ,,
Hayes, J., R.I.C.,   ,,
Howlin, Michael, W., Esq., High-street, Wexford.
Hynes, P., Esq., Bullring.
Hayes, John, Esq., John-street, Wexford.
Hore, Mrs. Ellen, Castle-street,   ,,
Holbrook, John, Esq., South Main-street, Wexford.
Harper, Matthew, Esq., North Main-street,   ,,
Hammond, A., Esq., Bridgetown.
Hammond, W., Esq.,   ,,
Harte, Thomas, Esq., Waterford.
Hanton, Robert, Esq., John-street, Wexford.
Hanrahan, P. J., Esq., Sydney.
Hore, Edmund, Chairman P.L.G., Wexford.
Hughes, Benjamin, Main-street, Wexford.
Hayes, Mr. Thomas, Coolawain.
Hanrahan, T., Somerset House, London.
Henry, Mitchell, M.P.
Healy, T. M., M.P., Dublin.
Harper, John Joseph, Esq., T.C., Wexford.
Hogan, John, Esq., H.M.I.R.
Hayes, Miss Ellen, Duncormack.
Hodson, Mr., M.A., Monck-street, Wexford.
Horan, James, Esq., Quay,   ,,
Hanrahan, John, Esq., Brisbane.
Hore James, Esq., Wexford.
Hanrahan, Mr. Patrick, Abbey-street, Wexford.
Harvey, William, Esq., Stonebridge.
Hayes, Peter, Esq., Ardcavan.
Hore, Rev. Simon B., O.S.F., Wexford.
Harper, Thomas, T.C.,   ,,

LIST OF SUBSCRIBERS.

Hanton, Gabriel, Esq., John-street, Wexford.
Harper, Moses, Esq., Main-street, ,,
Hanton, Peter, Esq., ,, ,,

I.

Irwin, John, Esq., W.H., Wexford.
Irwin, Mrs. Margaret, ,,

J.

Johnson, Charles, Esq., Tullybrook, Co. Donegal.
Jordan, Mr. John, Adamstown.
Jeffares, James J., Esq., Landscape.
Jeffares, W. E., A.B., St. Peter's College, Wexford.

K.

Kelly, Daniel, Esq., Enniscorthy.
Kelly, Mrs. D., ,,
Keating, Rev. James, C.C., Wexford.
Kelly, James Joseph, Esq., Main-street, Wexford.
Kavanagh, Very Rev. Michael, President St. Peter's College, Wexford.
Kelly, James, Esq., 61 Main-street, Wexford.
Kerwin, James, Esq., John-street, ,,
Keating, Mrs., Newtown, Co. Carlow.
Kerwin, Laurence, Esq., Bride-street, Wexford.
Kirwan, John, Esq., Mary-street, ,,
Kirwan, Laurence, Esq., John-street, ,,
Kirwan, James, Esq., ,, ,,
Kehoe, William, Esq., ,, ,,
Keating, Patrick, Esq., Prospect House, ,,
Keting, John, Esq., Moneyhore.
Kelly, Mr. Patrick, Cushinstown.
Kelly, Miss M., Caro.
Kelly, Mrs. Mary, Monck-street, Wexford.
Kehoe, Paul F., Esq., Moortown, Ballynulty.
Kelly, William J., Esq., Wexford.
Kelly, Rev. Michael, C.C., Manse, Wexford.
Kehoe, John J., Esq., North Main-street, Wexford.
Kelly, Michael, Esq., ,, ,, ,,
Kavanagh, Nicholas, Esq., ,, ,,
Kearns, Edward, Esq., Selskar.

LIST OF SUBSCRIBERS.

Keating, Nicholas, Esq., Elerslie.
Kehoe, Very Rev. P. D., O.S.F., Wexford.
Kehoe, James, P.L.G., Bregorteen.

L.

Lacy, Very Rev. J., P.P., Gorey (2 copies).
Lacy, Joseph, Esq., Wexford.
Lynch, Michl, Esq., Court-street, Enniscorthy.
Lyng, Rev. John, C.C., Blackwater.
Leary, Captain J., Trinity-street, Wexford.
Lawlor, William, Esq., John-street, ,,
Lyons, James, Esq., Port-Elizabeth, Cape Colony (50 copies).
Lambert, Rev. Walter, London.
Lennon, Mr. James, Inch, Borris, Co. Carlow.
Lennon, Mr. James, ,, ,,
Lennon, Mr. Patrick, Eden Vale, Castle Bridge.
Lynch, Mr. John B., Enniscorthy.
Lyons, Thomas J., Esq., Wexford.
Leigh, John Robert, Esq., Fairy Hill.
Long, Mr. Albert P., Bannow.
Long, Miss Kate, Ballindaggin.
Leary, James, Esq., Wexford.
Lennon, Rev. John, H.M., Enniscorthy.
Larkin, Miss Jane, John-street, Wexford.
Lambert, Patrick, Esq., H.C., Quay, Wexford.

M.

Murphy, Rev. Joseph, C.C., Evergreen Cottage, Ferns.
Martin, H. H., Esq., Wexford.
M'Clain, M., Esq., ,,
Marlow, J., Esq., Quay, Wexford.
Moore, James, Esq., Main-street, Wexford.
Murphy, Mr. P. J., Carrigbyrne.
Murray, Mr. Thomas, Co. Carlow.
Murphy, Mr. Owen, Trinity-street, Wexford.
Murphy, Francis, Esq., Faythe.
Murphy, Mr. William, Mary-street, Wexford.
Murphy, Nicholas, Esq., King-street, ,,
M'Grane, Michael, Esq., Ballintra, Co. Donegal.
M'Fadden, Rev. H., P.P., ,, ,,
M'Kay, Miss, B., Lahay, ,, ,,

LIST OF SUBSCRIBERS.

M'Carthy, Justin, M.P.
Murphy, Mr. Thomas, Ballynamonabeg.
Murphy, Mr. Daniel, High-street, Wexford.
Maddock, Patrick, Esq., Killeens.
Maher, Mrs. L. C., Ballinkeele (2 copies).
Murphy, Very Rev. W., Dean, Taghmon.
Murphy, Very Rev. Patrick, P.P., St. Anthony's, Liverpool.
Murphy, Hugh, Esq., Kilcullen.
Maddock, Rev. James, C.C., Newtownbarry.
Malons, David, Esq., Clareville, Finglas-road, Glasnevin, Co. Dublin.
Mullaly, Maurice, Esq., Supervisor, Excise.
Mangan, William, Esq., Monck-street, Wexford.
Marshall, Rev. Francis M., P.P.
M'Evoy, Miss Anastasia, Wexford.
Mayler, J. E., Esq., Harristown.
M'Donald, Mr. Patrick, Davidstown.
M'Donald, Mr. John, Wexford.
Murphy, Michael, Esq., ,,
Maddock, Mr. Michael, Glynn.
Moran, Mr. Luke, ,,
M'Carthy, Hugh, Esq., White's Hotel, Wexford.
Malone, William, Esq., Belvidere.
Murphy, Mr. William, Carrig.
Murphy, Miss Mary F., ,,
Mills, George, Esq., 3 Alfred-street, St. James's-road, Liverpool.
Macdonnell, Richard, Esq., Granard Villa, Wexford.
Murphy, Patrick, Esq., Castlebridge.
Meares, Thomas, R.I.C., ,,
M'Elwain, P., Esq., Lahay, Co. Donegal.
M'Dermott, M., Esq., Ballintra, ,,
Maguire, Mr. John, Enniscorthy.
M'Donald, Richard, Esq., Farycarrig.
Malowney, Richard, Esq., Selskar.
M'Carthy, J. J., architect, Westland-row, Dublin.
Mechanics' Institute, Wexford.
Murphy, Richard, Esq., King-street, Wexford.
Murphy George, Esq., High-street, ,,
Macawlay, T. P., Esq., Moyne House, Enniscorthy.

N.

Nolan, Felix, Esq., Wexford.

LIST OF SUBSCRIBERS.

O.

O'Connor, James, Esq., Wexford.
O'Neill, Mr. William, Kilmore.
O'Cavanagh, Thomas E., Limerick (2 copies).
O'Brien, Mr. Thomas, Monck-street, Wexford.
O'Callaghan, Mr. Patrick, Ballindaggin.
O'Callaghan, George L., Esq., London.
O'Callaghan, D. J., Esq., Newark, Notts.
O'Connor, Mr. Thomas P., School-street, Wexford.
Ogle, Thomas Acres, Esq., Verona, Enniscorthy.
O'Connor, John, Esq., Quay, Wexford.
O'Connor, Rev. Thomas, C.C.,　　　,,
O'Brien, Rev. James, C.C., Clareystown (2 copies).
O'Brien, Miss M. A., Ballyvaldon.
O'Connor, Miss Mary, Main-street, Wexford.
O'Connor, Mrs. E., Ailsbury-road, Donnybrook, Co. Dublin.
O'Donnell, Robert, Esq., Wexford.
O'Brien, Myles M., Esq., Tinabarna, Kilmuckridge.
O'Connor, Joseph, Esq., South Main-street, Wexford.
O'Meara, Daniel, Esq.,　　　,,　　　,,　　　,,
O'Connor, O. L., Esq., Port Louis, Mauritius.
O'Brien, Rev. John, P.P., Port-Elizabeth, Cape Colony.
O'Connor, Michael J., Esq., Wexford.
O'Keeffe, Thomas, T.C., Wexford.
O'Leary, Rev. P. M., C.C.,　　　,,
O'Connor, Rev. Patrick, St. Peter's College, Wexford.

P.

Peacocke, Charles H., Esq., Belmont House, Wexford.
Pierse, Thomas, M.D., Upper Rowe-street,　　　,,
Pierce, Bonadventure, Esq., architect,　　　,,
Power, Mr. Richard M., Brisbane, Queensland.
Power, Mr. James T., Shanbo', New Ross.
Pierce, Miss Margaret, Lough.
Pettit, William, Esq., Rathmore, Broadway.
Pierce, Philip, Esq., Folly Mills, Wexford.
Philips, Mr. Nicholas, Baldwinstown.

R.

Rowe, Mrs., Quay, Wexford.
Ryan, P. R., Esq., Enniscorthy.
Ryan, John, Esq., North Main-street, Wexford.
Ryan, Mr. Edward, Ballymurn.
Robert, Mrs., Rushbrook House, Wexford.
Rowe, Howard, Esq., Wexford.
Redmond, Mrs. P. W., Russel-street, Bath.
Robinson, William J., Esq., Wexford.
Ryan, Rev. M., C.C., Murrintown.
Rossiter, John J., Esq., London.
Redmond, George, Esq., Mary-street, Wexford.
Redmond, Moses, Esq., builder, Mary-street, Wexford.
Robinson, John D., Esq., Savannah, Georgia.
Ryan, Thomas P., Esq., Bury, Lancashire.
Roche, Rev. Thomas A., St. Peter's College, Wexford.
Rowe, Francis, Esq., Ralphtown House, ,,
Roche, Edward, Esq., Garralough House, ,,
Roche, Very Rev. Canon James, P.P., ,,
Ryan, E. T. G., Esq., Alma.
Ryan, G. O. B., Esq., Solicitor, Wexford.
Ryan, Patrick, Esq., Mullintra.
Roche, Mr. Richard, Kilmore (5 copies).
Ryan, Mr. William, Ballymurn.
Ryan, Miss J., ,,
Ryan, James N., Esq., Wexford.
Ryan, Patrick, Esq., West Gate.
Redmond, Mr. James, Screen.
Redmond, J. E., M.P., London.
Ryan, R. W., Esq., Solicitor, Wexford.
Ryan, Patrick, Esq., Ballygoman.
Reynolds, Rev. R., C.C., Clash, Cranford.
Ryan, Rev. James, C.C., Boolavogue.
Ryan, Richard, P.L.G., Wexford.
Roch, Mr. James, Abbey-street, Wexford.
Richards, John, Esq., Distillery House, Wexford.
Roche, Very Rev. Thomas, P.P., Lady's Island.
Richards, Thomas, H., Esq., Wexford.
Redmond, Thomas P., Esq., Clarence House, Wexford.
Redmond, Rev. D. W., C.C., Como Lodge, Castlebridge.

S.

Sheridan, Very Rev. P. C., P.P., Bannow.
Sullivan, T. D., M.P., Dublin.

LIST OF SUBSCRIBERS.

Sinnott, Walter, Esq., Castle-hill, Enniscorthy.
Story, William, Esq., High-street, Wexford.
Sinnott, Mr. John, Ballykelly, New Ross.
Scallan, William, Main-street, Wexford.
Summers, Matthew, Tommon Quay-street, Wexford.
Sinnott, Rev. Robert,, P.P., Ballycanew.
Sinnott, Alderman John, Wexford.
Sheridan, M. J., M.D., Wexford.
Stafford, Rev. John, O.S.F., Wexford.
Sinnott, John, Esq., Keerlogues.
Scallan, Francis, Esq., Slaney Hill, Wexford.
Stafford, Alderman Robert, Rockview, ,,
Sutherland, James W., Esq., Quay, ,,
Scallan, Miss Mary, Lough.
Scallan, Nicholas, Esq., Main-street, Wexford.
Stafford, Miss M. A., Glynn.
Stafford, James, Esq., North Main-street, Wexford.
Sinnott, John A., solicitor, Enniscorthy.
Snales, Richard G., Killashee.

T.

Talbot, John H., Esq., Castletalbot.
Tobin, Nicholas, Esq., Sea-view, Wexford.
Taylor, Charles, solicitor, The Castle, Wexford.

W.

Walsh, Edward, Mayor of Wexford.
Walsh, Richard, T.C., ,,
Walsh, Michael, Esq., Cornmarket, Wexford.
Whitmore, Miss Mary Jane, Taghmon.
Warley, Mrs. E., Wexford.
White, John, Esq., *People* Office, Wexford.
White, Michael, Esq., College-place, ,,
White, Nicholas, Esq., Anne-street, ,,
Walsh, Mr. Patrick, John-street, ,,
White, Miss A., Farmhouse, Bannow.
Walsh, Thomas, Esq., Coolcull.
Walsh, William, Esq., Kingstown (3 copies).
Walsh, Mrs. William, Rosbercon.
Walsh, Francis, Esq., Faythe.

LIST OF SUBSCRIBERS.

Wickham, Michael, Esq., Wexford.
Wright, James, Esq., Carrick, Co. Donegal.
Walsh, John, Esq., Carrig Lawn, Wexford.
Walsh, Jasper W., Esq., Summer Hill, Wexford
Walker, Robert, Esq.,   "
Walsh, Very Rev. John, P.P., Rathnure.

M. H. Gill and Son, Printers, Dublin.

www.ingramcontent.com/pod-product-compliance
Lightning Source LLC
Chambersburg PA
CBHW032353230426
43672CB00007B/687